When Grief Is Complicated

ALSO BY ALAN D. WOLFELT, PH.D., C.T.

Companioning the Bereaved:
A Soulful Guide for Caregivers

Companioning the Grieving Child:
A Soulful Guide for Caregivers

Companioning You!
A Soulful Guide to Caring for Yourself
While You Care for the Dying and the Bereaved

The Handbook for Companioning the Mourner:
Eleven Essential Principles

Reframing PTSD As Traumatic Grief:
How Caregivings Can Companion Traumatized
Grievers Through Catch-Up Mourning

Companion Press is dedicated to the education and support
of both the bereaved and bereavement caregivers. We believe that
those who companion the bereaved by walking with them as
they journey in grief have a wondrous opportunity:
to help others embrace and grow through grief—
and to lead fuller, more deeply-lived lives themselves
because of this important ministry.

For a complete catalog and ordering information, write, call, or visit:

Companion
P R E S S

The Center for Loss and Life Transition
3735 Broken Bow Road | Fort Collins, CO 80526
(970) 226-6050 | www.centerforloss.com

When Grief Is Complicated

A Model for Therapists to Understand,
Identify, and Companion Grievers Lost in
the Wilderness of Complicated Grief

ALAN D. WOLFELT, PH.D., C.T.

Companion Press is an imprint of the Center for Loss and Life Transition, 3735 Broken Bow Road, Fort Collins, Colorado 80526.

Companion Press books may be purchased in bulk for sales promotions, premiums, and fundraisers. Please contact the publisher at the above address for more information.

25 24 23 22 21 20 19 18   6 5 4 3 2 1

ISBN: 978-1-61722-258-0

*To the caregivers who have encouraged
me to add my voice to the mysterious body of
knowledge about complicated grief.*

*Without your support and inspiration, I would not
have written about applying the companioning
model of grief care to this critically important topic.*

Your enthusiasm has carried me as this resource unfolded.

Contents

Foreword

BY DONNA SCHUURMAN

It's no exaggeration to state that I've been waiting for this book for over a decade, and I believe Alan Wolfelt is the ideal person to have written it. As a clinical thanatologist with more than 30 years of in-the-trenches work with people grieving the deaths of loved ones (and sometimes not-so-loved ones), a training and speaking schedule fit for the Energizer Bunny, and a long list of publications to assist grievers, caregivers, and professionals alike, Alan represents the gold standard of care. He's introduced as an "expert" in the field of bereavement, and yet, over all these years and through all the tears of those he's witnessed, he understands fully that the real experts are the grieving children, teens, and adults themselves.

I first met Alan at a National Funeral Directors Association conference back in 1992, about a year after I accepted the position as Executive Director at The Dougy Center for Grieving Children and Families, in Portland, Oregon. As a newbie to the field, with a fresh doctorate in counseling and a small but dedicated staff serving bereaved children and their families, I eagerly lapped up advice and opinions from luminaries in the field. I joined the Association for Death Education and Counseling, read every book and journal I could get my hands on, and set about to grow our local services for grieving children as young as three and up through teens and young adults, as well as their often exhausted parents or adult caregivers. From those early days through the present, I resonated with Alan's model of "companioning" people through the difficult terrain of life after a death. Death is, after all, a universal experience, although our mainstream culture continues to avoid, derail, and deny its inevitability, often further complicating the already complex journey for people grappling with its finality and implications.

Around 1995 I started reading about researchers and clinicians seeking to identify high-risk grievers, variously referred to as suffering from "pathological grief" or "complicated grief," among a long list of symptom-related descriptors. The intention to study and understand how to better serve those who, after a death, may be at higher risk for negative outcomes is vitally important for those of us in helping professions of all kinds, whether clergy or counselors, psychologists or psychiatrists, social workers or school personnel. As I learned more and more from Dougy Center families, it became clear that their post-death lives often understandably included the ups and downs of sadness and depression, and sometimes regret and guilt, among a vast range of normal responses to the loss of parents and spouses and siblings and friends.

After a loss, some folks with preexisting emotional or behavioral issues found themselves sinking further into what felt like insurmountable terrain. We developed a robust referral list for those who needed more than our peer support groups offered, carefully vetting licensed professionals with training and experience specific to the needs of grieving children and/or adults. We found then, which is still true to this day, that most universities do not offer even one graduate course in grief and loss, a fact that continues to boggle my understanding. After all, every issue that propels a person to seek help involves loss, from loss of hope, loss of health, and loss of faith to relationship losses from abandonment, divorce, or death. My own doctoral program *in counseling* included roughly half an hour on death's impact on people, and yet we see people all around us suffering in deeper ways than they need to because of unaddressed grief and loss.

We also heard from our grieving youth and adults that their experiences were frequently made more painful due to the lack of understanding and support from the people around them. Family and friends they thought would "be there" for them disappeared or urged them to "move on." Coworkers avoided them, their social networks failed to include them, and even their places of worship neglected to minister to them after the compensatory early days of services or funerals.

As the move toward codifying "complicated grief" evolved into a top-down medical model with "symptoms" and timelines differentiating it from "normal grief," a new "mental disorder" related to grief was proposed for the *Diagnostic and Statistical Manual of Mental Disorders*, the *DSM*, published by the American Psychiatric Association. As you likely know, *DSM* codes are required in the U.S. to receive insurance reimbursement for "mental disorders," many of which in my view would be better addressed as "issues with being human" or "struggles of life." The proposal was rejected for inclusion in the *DSM-5* published in 2012, although a hybrid-term with its lists of symptoms was included under a section termed "Conditions for Further Study." Curiously named "Persistent Complex Bereavement Disorder," or PCBD, it is a "disorder" with symptoms even its advocates concede are all normal responses to loss through death. What propels it into a "mental disorder" is either/or the severity or duration of symptoms. Yet these criteria are social constructs, not scientific entities. As Alan points out in this book, "Complicated grief has proven such a challenging 'condition' to pin down precisely because it is, at its core, an ineffable, spiritual experience."

What Alan compellingly shares in these pages is, indeed, the work of a "responsible rebel" against a strong tide of those who seek to pathologize certain grieving people. I love that he is re-appropriating the term "complicated grief" from a Western medical mental disorder model to the reality that all grief is complicated, not simply because of what's going on in someone's head or mind, but also within their soul and our society. Grief is complicated because people and relationships are complicated, and when relationships end through death, these complex issues heighten in intensity. He's not asserting, nor am I, that every griever will be just fine in some la-la Pollyanna way. As The Dougy Center's peer support model grew from one little program in Portland, Oregon, to hundreds of programs throughout the U.S. and into other countries, I've been invited to assist grievers and communities following some of the most horrendous tragedies of our lifetimes. I've listened to the heartbreaking pain of parents whose six-year-olds were gunned down in their classroom, and the agony of Japanese families who lost loved ones and everything they owned in the 1993 and 2011 earthquakes. The issues they grapple with are complicated, intense, and lifelong. At the same time, their struggles ought not be pathologized as "mental disorders" needing "treatment" and "cure."

Whatever your training or degree, this book will provide you with principles and practical suggestions for helping grieving people. I'll be suggesting it as required reading for mental-health practitioners on our referral list at The Dougy Center, and I believe its revolutionary message will result in better understanding of and services for grieving people.

Donna Schuurman
Director of Advocacy & Training
Executive Director Emeritus
The Dougy Center for Grieving Children and Families
Portland, Oregon

Preface

A DECLARATION OF MY INTENT

Thank you for picking up this resource and being open to what we will be exploring together. While I have written a number of books over the years, this particular book was long in coming. Many of my colleagues and training participants have encouraged me to write a book on complicated grief for some time. However, I felt a need to wait, listen, and learn before I could attempt to express in words my unique perspective on companioning people with complicated grief. Yes, I'd presented workshops and intensive trainings for counselors, therapists, and educators on this topic many times. I had hoped to write a book about this important topic someday. Yet, I found myself postponing and even avoiding putting the pen to paper. In retrospect, I think I saved it until now because it was, in many ways, the most difficult book to write. I also firmly believe the waiting was part of my own maturational process.

That's because complicated grief is, well, complicated. And in my view, as you'll soon see, there is no simple, clear-cut, effective formula for therapists to use in helping grievers through it. Yes, there is an essential, mysterious body of knowledge to learn. By "mysterious body of knowledge," I mean both the many articles, books, studies, and case studies that have been so carefully crafted on this topic AND the fact that grief is mysterious and can never be fully explained. There is always more to learn and be open to.

There are, however, critical guiding principles. And there are definitely many people with complications of their grief who desperately need our compassionate help. In fact, as I was completing this book, we suffered another tragic school shooting—one in which the accused young man had a significant history of life losses. In addition, we have an entire world that needs reminding that grief and mourning are normal and necessary, especially when loss is complicated.

So, I finally summoned the perseverance to assemble in this primer what I have learned as a grief therapist over the last 35-plus years of walking with thousands of grievers. I hope you will reflect on my experience and put my unique perspective to good use in your work as a bereavement caregiver. I also hope you will seek out additional training on this topic and become one of the advocates working to make complicated grief care both more effective and more widely available.

My true prayer is that this book will be an invitation for you to create sacred spaces for your fellow human beings as they struggle with the natural complications that grief has brought into their lives. After all, the opportunity to connect with other people and help them discover ways to mourn well, live well, and love well is what the heart of caregiving is all about.

As you know, grief is anchored in heartbreak. The pain of loss has the power to disconnect us from our souls. As you offer yourself to others, I also want to gently remind you about the critical importance of your own self-care. So go forth, my friends and colleagues, with a well-tended spirit and an open heart.

Thank you for joining me in this conversation. I hope we meet one day.

Introduction

A 12-year-old boy's mother died in a car crash. His family, it turned out, wasn't so good at talking about death or openly mourning. Their unwritten rule went something like this: "Feeling sad won't bring her back. Be strong and carry on."

So the boy shut down all his emotions for many years. By the time he reached his 20s, he realized he was mad a lot of the time, though he didn't understand that his anger was related to the long-ago death. He said he often felt the need to punch someone. Many times he acted out and misbehaved in public and outrageous ways.

Finally, his older brother, who had also suffered, albeit more inwardly, encouraged the young man to see a therapist. In the safe harbor of his therapist's compassionate presence, he told his story. Over time, the walls he had built around his heart came tumbling down, and he finally began to embrace and express the grief he had carried for so long. He felt relief and reconciliation. His soul started to heal.

Together with his brother, the young man decided to share his experience of carried grief with the world. He knew that millions of people the world over might benefit from hearing their story. The brothers had suffered from complicated grief, and they wanted to raise awareness that it is common, it is understandable, and it can be identified. Most important of all, they wanted the world to know that trained grief companions can help guide complicated grievers move out of the shadows and into the light. There is help, and there is hope.

It's likely you've heard this story before. The 12-year-old boy was Prince Harry of Wales, and his older brother was Prince William. Their mother, of course, was Princess Diana. Harry and William's grief was complicated by many factors we will explore together in this book—including (but not limited to) a sudden, violent, untimely death; a closed family system; the magnifying glass of fame; and a challenging, at least for the family, funeral experience. And while their circumstances were somewhat unusual, in all the ways that count their complicated grief journeys were very much like everyone else's.

Harry and William had come to grief, as happens so often and so naturally throughout all our lives. They had suffered inside. They had run into barriers in their mourning. They had gotten stuck, and their quality of life was significantly diminished. They needed the companionship of a wise and caring therapist to help them get back on a healthy path to reconciliation.

While you may never companion grieving princes, you too are one of the special companions that complicated grievers from all walks of life so desperately need. This book is for you. Welcome.

A little context before we begin

Before we go any further, I would like to share with you a little about this book's genesis and point of view.

I am a traditionally trained psychologist. Several decades ago, I earned my Ph.D. in psychology. In my extensive schooling, I learned all the attendant rationales, methods, nomenclature, and conventions for diagnosing and treating mental-health issues as illnesses.

But my true area of interest was grief. Ever since I was a teenager, I knew I wanted to learn how to help people who had been wounded by loss. By the time I was 14, one of my young friends and both of my grandmothers had died, and I had personally experienced both profound grief and society's indifference to it. I was devastated. I felt sad, confused, and lonely, but I also noticed that nobody wanted to talk to me about the deaths. By the age of 16, I had decided that I would one day found the Center for Loss and Life Transition. I actually wrote my plan down on a napkin, and a number of years later saw that dream through to completion. Since then, I have spent four decades helping mourners, educating grief caregivers, writing books, and traveling the world to spread the word that if we help people mourn well, we help them go on to live and love well.

Most of my Ph.D. program colleagues continued on a clinical path in their careers, some in academia, some in private or institutional practice. I, too, began to see patients, but as quickly and as thoroughly as I could, I jettisoned the medical-model approach to grief and bereavement care and began using normalizing words and methods to help grievers. I became what I call a "responsible rebel."

Responsible rebel:

One who questions assumptive models surrounding grief and loss and challenges those very models. Rebels are not afraid to question established structures and forms. At the same time, responsible rebels respect the rights of others to use different models of understanding and provide leadership in ways that empower people rather than diminish them.

Why did I go rogue? Simply put: because I know that grief is not an illness. "Normal" grief is not an illness, and neither is complicated grief. (More on that shortly.) I don't believe in the medical model of diagnosing and treating people who mourn. Instead, I believe in "companioning" them, which is a philosophy of grief care based on the core tenets listed below.

Please note: Whenever you see a white number circled in black, as below, that means you'll find a corresponding handout for grievers in the Complicated Griever Educational Supplement. Details on pages 32 and 234.

The 11 tenets of companioning mourners

Following are my 11 basic principles of companioning, or caring for, people who are grieving. These tenets apply whether you are helping someone experiencing normal grief or complicated grief.

Tenet One:
Companioning is about being present to another person's pain; it is not about taking away the pain.

Tenet Two:
Companioning is about going to the wilderness of the soul with another human being; it is not about thinking you are responsible for finding the way out.

Tenet Three:
Companioning is about honoring the spirit; it is not about focusing on the intellect.

Tenet Four:
Companioning is about listening with the heart; it is not about analyzing with the head.

Tenet Five:
Companioning is about bearing witness to the struggles of others; it is not about judging or directing these struggles.

Tenet Six:
Companioning is about walking alongside; it is not about leading.

Tenet Seven:
Companioning is about discovering the gifts of sacred silence; it is not about filling up every moment with words.

Tenet Eight:
Companioning is about being still; it is not about frantic movement forward.

Tenet Nine:
Companioning is about respecting disorder and confusion; it is not about imposing order and logic.

Tenet Ten:
Companioning is about learning from others; it is not about teaching them.

Tenet Eleven:
Companioning is about compassionate curiosity; it is not about expertise.

Companioning is, in essence, a different way of looking at both grief itself and the caregiver's role in helping someone who is grieving. It is more art than science, more heart than head.

This book is the sixth I have written in my "Companioning Series" for caregivers. In 2006 I released *Companioning the Bereaved: A Soulful Guide for Caregivers*. In it I laid out my companioning model of grief care, exploring in some depth each of the companioning tenets as well as five other main principles that undergird my work. If you haven't already, I encourage you to read *Companioning the Bereaved* as an essential prequel to the book you hold in your hands.

In addition to *Companioning the Bereaved*, my "Companioning Series" includes books on companioning grieving children, counseling skills fundamentals for grief companions, self-care for grief companions, and PTSD as a form of complicated grief, as well as a brief primer on companioning called *The Handbook for Companioning the Mourner*.

I share this information with you by way of explaining how *When Grief is Complicated* fits into my body of work. If you are an advocate for or are at least curious about my companioning philosophy of bereavement care (as opposed to the medical model), this is not the only book you will want to read. Rather, it is a continuation of the companioning series and a more niche primer for those who find themselves in the position of companioning or referring complicated grievers in particular. And if you *have* already read my other companioning books, I thank you for bearing with me as I repeat in this book bits of the foundational material from other resources in the series.

Besides a deep dive into the companioning philosophy itself, what you will *not* find in this book is academic data or evidence-based analyses or studies. This book is more suggestive than prescriptive, more "consider this" than "do this." Companioning, you see, is more art than science, more heart than head. The topic at hand is "complicated grief"—a term appropriated by medical-model mental-healthcare practitioners. They commonly use it as a diagnosis of a pathology, mental illness, or disorder that needs to be treated and cured. I do not.

In my view, complicated grief is not an illness or disorder but instead a normal, human response to naturally complex life and loss circumstances. Yes, complicated mourners need help (that's where you come in), but they do not need clinical treatment or to be "cured." There's nothing "wrong" with them. They simply need compassionate understanding and gentle guidance to get back on track.

If you are a traditionally trained mental-healthcare practitioner, please know that I am well aware of the current in which you likely swim. Most caregivers go through their mental-health education with little or no training in bereavement care. Through no fault of your own, you may feel ill-prepared to help grievers, let alone complicated grievers. Alternately, you may have experience in— and feel allegiance to—the medical model of grief care. As you read this book, I simply ask that you consider my approach to grief care a supplement to your bereavement education. I hope this primer on complicated grief will enhance your understanding of the mysterious body of knowledge about grief and ultimately make you a more effective helper.

OK. That's me, and that's companioning. If my philosophy resonates with your own life and caregiving experiences, and if you want to learn more about how to companion complicated grievers, I invite you to continue.

First, what are grief and mourning? ❶

Grief is simply the term we use to describe our inner response to loss.

While grief is but a single word, the experience of grief encompasses a wide range of different thoughts and emotions. Essentially, grief is anything and everything we think and feel inside when we are separated from something or someone we are attached to.

We grieve when someone we love dies, yes. But we also grieve when we divorce, relocate, or separate from a job we are attached to, among many other common life losses, large and small.

And since loss is a normal and unavoidable part of life, our natural human response to loss is also normal. Grief is natural and necessary.

Here's another way of thinking about it: Grief is love's conjoined twin. Grief is what we feel when we are separated from the object of our love. Without love there would be no grief. And if love is not an illness or diagnosis, then neither is grief.

What's more, just like love, grief is primarily a deeply emotional as well as, I believe, spiritual journey. It transcends time and place. It is mysterious and ineffable. We prize love above every other human experience not just because it is joyful but because it is supremely meaningful, imbuing grief with the same sense of purpose and gravitas. And what survives death, according to various religions and billions of people? Most of us assuage our grief in part with the hope that our souls will one day be reunited with the souls of those who have gone before us. Grief, like love, dwells in the heart and soul, making grief a soul-based journey.

What about non-loving relationships and grief?

While grief and love/attachment usually go hand-in-hand, and you will find I use phrases such as "death of someone loved" and "loved one" throughout this book, I would be remiss if I did not also clearly state up-front that not all relationships that engender grief are anchored in love. Abusive, ambivalent, and difficult relationships are also risk factors for complicated grief. Sometimes absent relationships are as well, because it is human nature to grieve for what might have been. After a death, people often grieve what they never had but always longed for in a relationship. Please keep this important caveat in mind as you continue reading. It is a good reminder to always let each unique griever teach you about the nature of the love—or lack thereof—he experienced in a relationship he is grieving.

But what is mourning, then? Mourning is grief gone public. It's the outward expression of our grief. It's our shared social response to loss. Whenever we cry, talk about our grief, or in any way express our anger, sadness, shock, or any other thought or feeling about a loss, we're mourning.

Mourning, too, is normal and natural. After all, we're born crying! And as we move through childhood, we continue to cry and wail and protest whenever something we care about is taken away from us. In other words, we mourn. And mourning, like grief, is necessary. Mourning helps us reconcile our grief and find our way to a new normal.

Unfortunately, here in the West, our society believes that mourning is unseemly. We are pressured to keep our grief inside of us. Spoken or unspoken, messages such as "Be strong and carry on," "Don't look back; move forward," and "Being sad doesn't help" prevail. That's why I and others often refer to North America as a predominantly "mourning-avoiding culture."

I would say that even the inner experience of grief has been tainted by this thinking. We are told we have a right to happiness. We are told that emotional and spiritual pain are bad and that we deserve to quell them as quickly as possible. But if sadness is maladaptive, then grief is also maladaptive, right?

No wonder we ended up with grief and mourning too often being considered illnesses.

Complicated grief and mourning ❶

My professional experience has taught me that complicated grief is simply normal, necessary grief that has gotten stuck or off track somehow. It has encountered barriers or detours of one kind or another, and as a result has become stalled, waylaid, or denied altogether. It is *not* abnormal or pathological. Instead, it is a normal response in what is almost always an abnormally challenging loss situation.

The medical modelers of the grief world, conversely, believe that complicated grief is a disorder. In the next section I will briefly summarize the history of modern psychology's understanding of complicated grief. This review will further elucidate the ways in which the medical model of complicated grief and my companioning model of complicated grief part company.

Remember, grief is what we naturally think and feel inside after a loss, so for me, complicated grief is a naturally complicated inner experience of grief. Denied, or "carried," grief also falls into this category, as does grief in which any particular feature predominates for a long period of time.

Let me also be clear that I believe *all* grief is complicated. Just as love is always complex and multifaceted, so too is grief. Whenever someone we love dies, we naturally have lots of different and ever-changing thoughts and feelings about the death. Grief is often profoundly challenging and chaotic. In fact, it's common for grievers to feel like they're going crazy because their inner experience of loss is so different from their usual thoughts and feelings. The experience we're calling "complicated grief" in this book is simply regular old complicated grief that's gotten *extra* complicated somehow. It's a matter of degree, feature prominence, functional impact, and sometimes duration.

Complicated mourning, on the other hand, is a behavioral or outward manifestation of complicated grief. Substance abuse is a common type of complicated mourning. Self-harming would be another. So would aggression, OCD patterns, or visible depressive symptoms. You will find that in this text I sometimes use the terms complicated grief and complicated mourning interchangeably, because both are often present at the same time, but when a distinction is called for, I will note it.

A history of modern psychology's understanding of complicated grief

Allow me a moment to dip into the distant past before outlining the more modern academic view of complicated grief.

Over the course of human history, different cultures have embraced or eschewed grief in different ways and developed norms that we still see vestiges of today. The ancient Greeks publicly lamented the dead and believed that the deceased's immortality hinged on his continued remembrance by the living. Throughout the Middle Ages and the Renaissance period, Europeans wore mourning clothing (white in medieval times; black in later centuries) to publicly demonstrate their ongoing, long-term grief. Some Victorian-era cemeteries in the United States were designed as public parks, in the hopes of integrating the living and the dead.

In fact, throughout recorded human history and across cultures, prolonged and visible mourning was not only normalized, it was encouraged. Customs and mores often provided structures and extended timetables in recognition of the reality that grief not only lasts a good long while, it requires public support and recognition, and it must take priority in mourners' lives.

It wasn't until the 1900s, and especially in America, that pronounced or prolonged mourning began to be pathologized.

We may have Dr. Sigmund Freud to thank for that. He was the first prominent thinker to propose a theory of complicated grief. A hundred years ago, in his famous 1917 paper "Mourning and Melancholia," he claimed a distinction between normal mourning and "**melancholia**," which he understood as a pathological response to loss. He described the distinguishing features of melancholia as follows:

> …a profoundly painful dejection, cessation of interest in the outside world, loss of the capacity to love, inhibition of all activity, and a lowering of the self-regarding feelings to a degree that finds utterance in self-reproaches and self-revilings, and culminates in a delusional expectation of punishment.

Still, in the same paper he went on to say that with the exception of the diminishment of self-regard, the same features overlapped with normal mourning. More discussion of possible nuanced differences followed, and Freud concluded that the main distinction lay in the realm of the ego and the "pathological mourner's" possible devolvement into self-hatred and possibly suicide. We'll talk more about damaged self-esteem and suicidal ideation later, but I agree with Freud—they are likely the two most concerning symptoms.

As you know, Freud was a psychiatric generalist; he studied and became famous for his thinking about a wide range of mental-health issues. But by the 1940s, we began to see professionals specializing in bereavement, the psychiatrist Dr. Erich Lindemann among them. He differentiated between what he called normal grief and "**morbid grief**," claiming that the hallmarks of morbid grief were delayed reactions to the loss (weeks to years) and distorted reactions, such as changes in relationships with others, hostility against certain people (a doctor who treated the person who died, for example), and loss of social interaction. I agree that both delayed and distorted reactions may indicate complicated grief, but they are also common in normal grief.

In my training, I found myself agreeing with child psychiatrist Dr. John Bowlby's theory of attachment. In 1961, he emphasized that grief is an instinctive and universal reaction to separation from the object of the attachment. He defined several types of "disordered attachment," including "anxious attachment," i.e., insecure and overly dependent attachment, which he believed tended to result in **chronic grief**. His research helped us understand a truth: The nature of the relationship the griever had with the person who died always has a significant influence on her grief.

As early as 1970, Dr. Aaron Lazare described what he called "**unresolved grief**," listing symptoms such as an unwillingness to move the possessions of the deceased after a reasonable amount of time, guilt and self-reproach, and changes in current relationships—all, I would add, common symptoms in normal grief. What's more, I do not believe that grief is ever "resolved;" instead, people learn to integrate it into their sense of self and continue on with life even as they know that their grief will never truly end. In this manner, all grief is unresolved. Complicated grief may be particularly *unreconciled*, but that is a distinction we will discuss in Part Three.

Researchers began studying the biology of grief as early as the 1970s. Over the decades, several study results have shown that grievers in general have depressed immune function and heightened inflammatory response. Cortisol levels are also dysregulated. We'll talk more about the neurobiological correlates of grief in Part Three as they relate to "treatment" options, but for now I'll just say that while grief lives in the body, it is my firm belief that it is a condition of the soul.

In 1993, my colleague and psychotherapist Dr. Therese Rando published a beefy textbook called *Treatment of Complicated Mourning*. In it she defined complicated mourning in this way: "...given the amount of time since the death, there is some **compromise, distortion, or failure of one or more of the six "R" processes of mourning**"—

- Recognize the loss
- React to the separation
- Recollect and re-experience the deceased and the relationship
- Relinquish the attachment
- Readjust to the new world
- Reinvest

My thinking about complicated mourning and how mourners heal is actually similar to Dr. Rando's, but I eschew the clinical framework of diagnosis and treatment.

By 1995, Dr. Holly Prigerson, now a professor of psychiatry at Harvard Medical School, was devising and testing an Inventory of Complicated Grief, which asked patients to answer 22 questions targeted at the most "**maladaptive" grief symptoms** (those that were thought to predict "enduring functional impairment"), such as "I feel the urge to cry when I think about the person who died" and "I feel disbelief over what happened." For each question, grievers were asked to report a frequency of 0 (never) to 4 (always). A certain score indicated complicated grief.

In 1997, Dr. Mardi Horowitz, a professor of psychiatry at the University of California—San Francisco, proposed criteria for "**complicated grief disorder.**" His research indicated that having at least three of the following seven symptoms at 14 months after the death and beyond "in a severity that interferes with daily functioning" is diagnostic: unbidden memories or intrusive fantasies related to the lost relationship; strong spells or pangs of severe emotion; distressingly strong yearnings or wishes that the deceased were there; feelings of being far too much alone or personally empty; excessively staying away from people, places or activities that remind the subject of the deceased; unusual levels of sleep interference; and loss of interest in work, social, caretaking, or recreational activities to a maladaptive degree.

A grief by any other name

Throughout the decades, the terminology used to label complicated grief has been debated. The following terms have all been considered:

- *abnormal grief*
- *chronic grief*
- *morbid grief*
- *pathological grief*
- *persistent complex bereavement disorder*
- *prolonged grief disorder*
- *traumatic grief*

The most prominent medical-model researchers have yet to achieve consensus on a term. Again, I strongly believe that grief is never abnormal, morbid, or pathological, nor is it ever a disorder. Instead, it is the normal and necessary sequel to having loved. What's more, grief is naturally endless.

So many individual and cultural variations exist in grief norms that it is challenging to easily and clearly say "this is normal grief" and "this is abnormal grief." The truth is that grief responses fall on a reverse bell curve. The interesting thing about this continuum is that grief responses on either side of the curve are usually forms of complicated grief—absent (or unembarked) grief on the one side and exaggerated (or encamped) grief on the other.

I have decided to use the term "complicated grief" in this book because it most closely aligns with my understanding of the experience. It acknowledges a grief that has encountered especially high hurdles of one kind or another. Medical-model clinicians and their literature often use the shorthand "CG" for complicated grief, but I will not because I believe the acronym is reductive and unempathetic.

In 2008, researchers were beginning to see what complicated grief looks like in the brain. In a seminal study, Mary Frances O'Connor, at UCLA, put grieving women in MRI scanners—some who seemed to be experiencing normal grief and some whose grief was prolonged and heightened. While in the scanner, the women were shown photos of the people who died or words associated with the death. The brains of both groups showed activity in pain-related neurological circuits, but the complicated grievers' brains also lit up in an area called the *nucleus accumbens*—which is a reward center known to activate in addicts when they view images of their drug of choice. The thinking was that the complicated grievers still had **unusually strong attachments** to the loved ones who had died, though others posited that complicated grievers may be addicted to their grief. Since then, further imaging studies have implicated a **dysfunction of the *rostral anterior cingulate cortex*, which regulates emotion**, in complicated grief. Such findings are interesting and valid. Love's sojourns in the brain have also been studied, but as far as I know, we are not using the brain science of love to try to manipulate the experience of love. Why would we use it to try to manipulate the experience of grief?

By 2009, Drs. Prigerson and Horowitz and their teams had joined together to create a unified understanding of diagnostic complicated grief symptoms. Calling the new diagnosis "**prolonged grief disorder**," the researchers determined that at least six months after the death, patients must exhibit yearning for the person who died as well as five of the following nine symptoms at least daily or to a disturbing degree (impairing their ability to function in daily life): avoidance of reality of the loss; emotional numbness; feeling stunned; feeling that life is meaningless; confusion of identity; mistrust; difficulty accepting the loss; bitterness over the loss; and difficulty moving on with life.

I simply do not believe that grief can be scored in such a way. Can we assign a number on a scale to someone's love for or relationship with another human being? No. It seems obvious to me that neither love nor grief submit to numerical analysis. As sociology professor William Bruce Cameron famously wrote, "Not everything that can be counted counts, and not everything that counts can be counted."

Meanwhile, Dr. Katherine Shear, at Columbia University's Center for Complicated Grief, became another important voice in the professional literature—a voice that I believe has a more nuanced and perhaps less disease-oriented approach to complicated grief. Her studies have indicated that "complicated grief is best understood as an unusually severe and prolonged form of acute grief rather than a completely unique entity." She also said, "Intense grief is not pathologic; however, complicating thoughts and behaviors that impede adaptation to the loss should be identified along with grief that is inordinately intense and prolonged." She also supports the use of a semi-structured interview by clinicians as well as a scored self-inventory of symptoms as a screening tool.

To this day, Drs. Horowitz, Prigerson, Shear, and others continue to wrestle over nomenclature, diagnostic criteria for complicated grief, assessment tools, and codification of a diagnosis to be included in the *Diagnostic and Statistical Manual* (more on that in a minute). They are conducting studies, publishing research, and writing articles for the likes of *The New England Journal of Medicine, World Psychiatry*, and the National Institutes of Health. Pains have also been taken to try to separate out complicated grief from post-traumatic stress disorder and clinical depression.

While I value their contributions and agree that there are likely millions of mourners out there who need extra support, I believe that when it comes to complicated grief, the researchers are barking up the wrong tree. I understand the desire to help as many people as efficiently as possible through research and data analysis. But I also know that complicated grief has proven such a challenging "condition" to pin down precisely because it is, at its core, an ineffable, spiritual experience. Like love, its twin, grief cannot be weighed and measured. Complicated grief is too complicated to be addressed with a manualized, one-size-fits-all therapeutic approach. Rather, grief can only be felt and expressed, and only the arts of empathy and grief companionship can help when grief gets stuck or off-trail.

Diagnostic codes and criteria

While all this discussion has been going on, the *Diagnostic and Statistical Manual*, or *DSM*, has captured psychiatrists' thinking about grief in the years that it was published and later updated— the first *DSM*, in 1952; the *DSM-II*, in 1968; the *DSM-III*, in 1980; the *DSM-IV*, in 1994; the *DSM-IV-TR*, in 2000; and the still-new *DSM-5*, in 2013.

Before the *DSM-III*, bereavement was not included in the *DSM*, and thus it wasn't technically part of mental-health caregivers' diagnostic purview. Starting with the *DSM-III*, depression after the death of a loved one was considered normal grief and not clinical depression unless certain severe symptoms were present (such as guilt, suicidal thoughts, worthlessness, marked functional impairment, or psychosis) or the depression lasted longer than two months. Yet I know that passive suicidal thoughts are common among grievers, self-esteem often suffers, and the normal depression of grief quite often lasts longer than two months. The recursive nature of grief invites normal waves of grief that often bring about being "pressed down" more in the months after the death.

The *DSM-IV-TR* added a distinction between normal and pathological grief. Pathological bereavement symptoms are defined as guilt about things other than actions taken or not taken by the survivor at the time of the death, thoughts of death other than the survivor feeling that she would be better off dead or should have died with the deceased person, morbid preoccupation with worthlessness, marked psychomotor retardation, prolonged and marked functional impairment, and hallucinatory experiences other than the griever thinking he hears the voice of or transiently sees the deceased person. It was further noted that the duration and expression of normal bereavement varies from cultural group to cultural group. Do you see how the thinking is getting more nuanced? This is good, but it is still too prescriptive. Lots of mourners, for example, feel guilt or regret about things other than actions taken or not taken at the time of the death.

Before the *DSM-5*, depression that followed the death of a loved one excluded someone from being diagnosed with clinical depression after just two weeks' duration of symptoms except in cases of suicidal thoughts, psychosis, or extreme impairment in everyday functioning. Now, under the *DSM-5*, this "bereavement exclusion" has been removed. Thus, the normal and necessary depression of grief can now be diagnosed as clinical depression as little as *two weeks* (!!!) after a death.

To be fair, the *DSM-5* also includes guidelines to help the clinician distinguish between ordinary grief and major depression. For example, the manual makes note of the fact that grieving people are often able to feel a variety of feelings, including not just sadness but also happier emotions, while depressed people feel stuck in sadness. Depressed people feel pain constantly, whereas grieving people experience their pain in waves. And grieving people have hope for the future, whereas depressed people feel hopeless.

These distinctions are helpful, but I am among the many grief counselors who believe that the *DSM-5* is a dangerous step toward characterizing grief as a medical condition that should be treated away instead of a normal and necessary spiritual journey that is healed over the course of months and years through active and ongoing mourning.

In its "Areas for Further Study," the *DSM-5* now includes a category called Persistent Complex Bereavement Disorder, formerly known as Complicated Grief Disorder, as well as diagnostic checklists for youths and for adults. Symptoms mirror those of normal grief—such as numbness, rumination about the circumstances or consequences of the death, anger, avoidance of reminders of the deceased or seeking out reminders—but also at least one of the following: intense and persistent yearning for the deceased, frequent preoccupation with the deceased, intense feelings of emptiness or loneliness, recurrent thoughts that life is meaningless or unfair, and frequent urge to join the deceased in death. (Dr. Shear and her team have proposed an alternate, more nuanced set of criteria.)

The international correlate of the *DSM* is the *International*

Statistical Classification of Diseases and Related Health Problems, or *ICD*, produced by the World Health Organization. The *ICD-10-CM* diagnostic code F43.21 "adjustment disorder with depressed mood" includes complicated bereavement and grieving, but the organization is also moving to introduce a new diagnosis called "Prolonged Grief Disorder."

So do I think complicated grief should be included in the *DSM* and *ICD*? Yes, but not because I agree that complicated grief is a true disorder or mental illness. Under our current healthcare system here in the United States, a formal diagnosis is required for treatment reimbursement. If people struggling with complicated grief are to receive the help of professional grief companions, a formal diagnosis is necessary.

The trouble is, of course, when we give grievers a diagnosis, they believe that something is wrong with them. They believe they're not grieving properly. They think we're the experts of their grief instead of them. They feel ashamed. They think, as our medicalized world has taught them, that they need to be treated and "cured." And we, in turn, often internalize the belief that we are the experts who hold the key to their "recovery."

Nothing could be further from the truth.

3 I encourage you to share the grief companion's view of therapy with the complicated grievers in your care. If you explain to them that they are not ill or suffering from a disorder, they will feel more empowered and capable from the beginning of their therapy experience. Perhaps one day psychiatrists, other providers, and insurers will agree that people do not have to be ill or disordered to be in need of support. In the meantime, we will have to live with the *DSM* and *ICD* stratifications, assessment scores, and nomenclature, though I offer my glossary as an alternative.

Glossary of terms ❹

Words are powerful. I provide this glossary as a quick reference to the terms I prefer to use both professionally, among colleagues, and in conversation with complicated grievers.

carried grief—grief from earlier in life that was never mourned

clean pain—the normal and necessary hurt of loss

clinical depression—depression characterized by a depressed mood and/or lack of pleasure as well as other symptoms, particularly a low sense of self-worth and the inability to function day-to-day

companioning—my philosophy of grief counseling; the art of empathetic walking alongside those in grief instead of "treating" them

complicated grief—normal grief that is stuck or has strayed off course and is not softening over time but instead becoming entrenched or worsening—almost always due to complicated loss circumstances. Not "pathological" or a mental illness or disorder but instead a normal, understandable response to abnormally challenging loss circumstances.

dirty pain—the compounding or distorting of the hurt of loss by worrying about "what ifs" or catastrophizing

divine spark—each human being's soul or essence

dosing pain—embracing hurt a bit at a time, allowing the griever to retreat and take a break before approaching it again

grief—everything people think and feel inside when they experience a loss *mourning*—when grievers express their grief outside themselves

perturbation—when grievers embrace, explore, and express their thoughts and feelings, which allows them to change and soften; emotions in motion

reconciliation—when grievers have integrated their grief into their continuing lives and are able to once again live and love fully, though they also understand that their grief will never truly end

symptoms—In grief, I think of symptoms as care-eliciting mourning manifestations of grief. They are not signs of an illness but instead normal and necessary signals that help the griever and others, including caregivers, understand that the griever is wrestling with grief and needs support.

The wilderness of complicated grief

For several decades now, I have spoken and written of grief as a wilderness experience. I've found that this is a metaphor that grievers understand and relate to, and I will be using it in this book as well.

When we think of grief as an arduous journey through a vast, inhospitable, mountainous forest, we capture some of the essence of the normal, necessary experience. Traversing grief is challenging. We don't always know where we're going. It's easy to lose the trail. We sometimes feel the warmth of the sun and glimpse great beauty, but we often encounter obstacles and dangers we weren't expecting. We're not always as well-equipped as we thought or wish we were, and we definitely cannot control the forces swirling around us. Understandably, we get tired. Along the way, it gets dark, stormy, and slippery, and though we'd often like to be able to fast-forward ourselves to the end of the trail, the only way out is through.

If every significant grief journey is such a challenging trek through the wilderness, what is complicated grief? It's an even more challenging odyssey. Here in Colorado we're privileged to be home to numerous 14,000-foot Rocky Mountain peaks, or 14ers, as they're called. Because of the terrain and topography, some of our 14ers are particularly difficult to summit. They remind me of complicated grief—rugged, relentless, and vast.

Hikers often get lost in or stranded on Colorado's mountain trails and peaks, and when this happens, we as a community take it quite seriously. After all, these travelers are often in mortal danger. Predators such as mountain lions lurk in the shadows, and the cold, wind, altitude, and vertiginous drops make unassisted survival unlikely. The backcountry is unforgiving.

Fortunately for the lost hikers, Colorado has teams of volunteers and professionals at the ready to locate and retrieve them. These search-and-rescuers are well-trained and well-equipped for the often perilous expeditions. More often than not, the endangered hikers live to tell the tale. They are forever changed by their wilderness experience, but they are able to continue on with their lives with gratitude and new perspective.

Companioning others through complicated grief is not unlike search and rescue. Well-trained volunteers and professionals are called upon to assist when we are alerted that a griever is struggling in the wilderness. It is our job to join them—to meet them where they are—and to accompany them back to safety. While it is not the grief companion's role to carry, lead, or find the way out, it is our responsibility to bear witness, provide shelter, offer sustenance, carry tools, safeguard vital signs, and imbue hope. We are not rescuers in the saver or savior sense; rather, we are rescuers in the "thank goodness you were here to help me" sense.

In short, some people get lost or trapped in the jeopardous

wilderness of their naturally complicated grief. We find them and help walk them back to safety. I believe this ministry is nothing less than search-and-rescue of the human soul, and I am honored to lead you in this discussion. Thank you for entrusting me with your time and attention.

Why all of this matters

Dr. Shear believes that as much as three percent of the population may experience complicated grief. Other researchers posit that the number is closer to ten to fifteen percent. When you consider that complicated grief is more of a continuum than a yes-no, and you give thought to all the people affected by the risk factors we'll be reviewing in Part One, it's easy to imagine that the true incidence could be much, much higher.

All grievers need the support of people who care about them, but complicated grievers usually need some professional support and guidance to help them get back on track. If they don't receive the help they need, they often become stuck in their misery, emptiness, or harmful behavior. They remain lost in the wilderness. They die while they are alive.

Not only are people lost in the wilderness of complicated grief unable to self-actualize, they often stultify or negatively affect others around them. Their partners and children can be hurt by their ongoing complicated grief. Their colleagues and neighbors can suffer. And the potential they brought with them into this world is never realized. In essence, their quandary sends ripples out into the world, as each person's life they touch affects the next person and so on and so on and so on.

Complicated grievers need you. The world needs you. The good news is that with a body of mysterious knowledge and companioning skills, you can indeed help.

How to use this book

In addition to the Introduction, this book contains three sections. Part One is a review of the risk factors for complicated grief. Part Two is a rundown of common symptoms of complicated grief. And Part Three offers guidance and ideas on caring for complicated grievers, based on my decades of professional experience.

At the end of each section are questions I invite you to answer. The questions are geared to help you not only review and remember the information you've just read, but also begin to integrate it with your own experience caring for complicated grievers. While, as I've said, this primer is more suggestive than prescriptive, I do hope you will begin putting its principles to use right away.

You will also see this symbol here and there throughout this book (including earlier in this chapter): **❶**. This indicates content that it is necessary for you to educate grievers about, both in general and as it concerns them in particular. To assist you in your educational and companioning role, I have created a series of griever handouts and worksheets and packaged them together in a Complicated Grief Educational Supplement. This 8.5 x 11-inch 50-page PDF is available for purchase and download on www.centerforloss.com. For your ease of use, the professionally designed handouts and forms included in the supplement are numbered, and whenever a symbol appears in this book, the number indicates the particular handout that corresponds to the adjacent content. I hope you will print out handouts and forms from the supplement and use them as appropriate with the grievers in your care.

Questions for reflection and understanding

In a notebook or computer file, I invite you to answer the provided questions at the end of each section of this book. Writing down your thoughts will help you understand and remember the concepts as well as integrate them with your unique methods of helping grievers.

What was I taught about grief during my education and professional training?

What are the main lessons I have learned on my own since I started caring for grievers professionally?

How do I define grief and mourning?

How do I define complicated grief? What is the difference between normal grief and complicated grief?

What questions do I have about complicated grief?

What do I think about the medical model of grief care?

What do I think about the companioning model of grief care?

What are my hopes and goals for my grief therapy practice moving forward?

PART ONE

Understanding the Origins of Complicated Grief

So, how is that some people end up in a wilderness of grief that is more rugged and perilous than the wildernesses of others? Why are some grief terrains more treacherous? In other words, how do some people's grief journeys get extra complicated?

In the Introduction we reviewed various definitions of complicated grief, historical and current. I contrasted the medical-model understanding of complicated grief as a disorder with my belief that complicated grief is a normal, human, soul-based response to naturally complex life and loss circumstances.

Here in Part One, we'll take a look at those naturally complex life and loss circumstances, which range from cultural contributors to circumstances of the death, the griever's relationship with the person who died, family systems influences, the funeral experience, and many others. These are the variables that—alone or, more often, in combination with one another—commonly result in complicated grief. They may form, if you will, the especially formidable topography of complicated grief.

Throughout this section, you will also find snippets of examples representing the voices of actual complicated grievers whom either I or caregivers who have participated in my trainings have companioned. In all cases, I have made an effort to minimize identifying details and protect confidentiality.

As we go over each of the influences on complicated grief, let's remember that "normal" grief and complicated grief are not truly distinct responses. Rather, we have agreed to understand complicated grief as normal grief—which by its very nature is always complicated—that has gotten *extra* complicated somehow. It's a matter of degree, feature prominence, functional impact, and, sometimes, duration.

In other words, there is not one backpack labeled "normal grief" and one labeled "complicated grief." We cannot separate them from one another nearly so neatly (though, as we discussed in the Introduction, I am well aware that the diagnosis "complicated grief" is the very thing that often allows grievers to receive the professional help they need and be reimbursed by their health insurance plans). There are simply grievers who, at some point in their journeys, are struggling to the degree that they would really benefit from the support of a trained grief companion. (I would further note that most grievers, at some point in their journeys, would likely be helped along by compassionate counseling, though it is often unnecessary for those with strong family and/or peer support.)

Complicated grief influences and risk factors

Please keep in mind that the grief influences and risk factors we are about to review together do not *necessarily* result in complicated grief. For example, multiple concurrent stressors is one of the influences that may contribute to complicated grief, but for various reasons, not everyone in seemingly high-stress circumstances will end up becoming lost or stuck in the wilderness of complicated grief.

Therefore, please do not think of the items in this section as

a checklist or formula of any kind but instead merely a list of
possible **risk factors.**

Also, it is possible that in your companioning practice you will end up working with grievers who do not appear to have any of the risk factors I list in this section yet who seem to be experiencing complicated grief. When this happens, do not fret! Human life, love, and grief are funny like that. There are simply not always clear causes or reasons for emotional and spiritual soul-based experiences. Love is mysterious, and so too is grief.

The bottom line is this: if someone in the wilderness of grief needs search and rescue, she needs search and rescue. Your job is to meet her where she is, provide a sacred and safe space, listen deeply with intent to understand, normalize without minimizing, and empathize without judgment. As each griever shares her story, at her own pace, you will be listening for these risk factors, of course, to aid in your understanding and to help you discern how best to help her get back on an effective path, but more important, you will be bearing witness to and honoring her unique love and grief. The complex mix of reasons *why* her unique love and grief are as they are is less important than accepting them at face value and accompanying her forward from there.

The below list of complicated grief influences and risk factors is numbered for ease of reference, but do not misconstrue that it is ranked. I have not presented the influences in any particular order. What's more, this list is not meant to be exhaustive, but it does represent the influences and risk factors I have seen most often in my many years as a grief counselor and educator. You may encounter others that are not included here. (If you do, I hope you will write to me about them at drwolfelt@centerforloss.com. I may have the opportunity to include your insights in a future article or book chapter.)

1. SOCIETAL CONTRIBUTORS

The remainder of the possible influences on complicated grief in Part One apply to the individual griever's unique loss circumstances, but this influence affects many if not most of us. At least here in America, we live in a culture in which many people do not "do" death and grief. And when death and grief are taboo, as they are here, our normal and necessary mourning is often stigmatized and suppressed. Our grief is, as Lutheran minister and professor of gerontology Dr. Kenneth Doka coined, "disenfranchised." In other words, our natural impulse to grieve and mourn is taken away from us.

How did this happen? First, we live in the **world's first death-free generation**. In centuries past, aging, illness, and death were much more a part of everyday life. Most people routinely suffered the (often premature) deaths of many loved ones. Today, many of us now live into our 40s or 50s before experiencing a close personal loss. Today two-thirds of all deaths in the U.S. each year happen to people who are 65 or older. While we certainly appreciate the medical advances that have helped lower the mortality rate and prolong lifespans, they have also distanced us from the normalcy of death and grief.

Second and relatedly, **we have moved aging, illness, and death off-stage** and hidden them where we can't see them. Hospitals, nursing homes, and funeral homes were largely inventions of the 20th century. Before they became prevalent, families cared for their aged and ill loved ones at home. Death occurred in the home, and families prepared and sat vigil over the bodies of their dead loved ones at home. Young people learned the customs of grief and mourning—which included public expression of grief, use of ritual, and ample social support—at their parents' knees. Now, death and grief are considered unseemly, even morbid, and we have forgotten the extended, public, and ritualized norms that served us so well.

Third, **we misunderstand the role of pain and suffering**. Our Puritanical heritage has imbued in us the misconception that sorrow is self-indulgent, and modern medicine has taught us that pain is unnecessary. Whenever we experience pain, we simply need to take a pill or undergo some kind of treatment, and just like that, no more pain. Our Declaration of Independence even promises us the right to the pursuit of happiness. Grief is normal and necessary pain, but when pain is vilified, so is grief. And while this closeting of grief affects everyone, **men** have been especially subject to its edicts. Crying and talking openly about feelings and loss have long been considered unmanly. These and many other common misconceptions about grief and loss contribute to the incidence of complicated grief.

Common grief misconceptions that may contribute to complicated grief ❿

When grievers have, knowingly or unknowingly, internalized some or all of these prevalent misconceptions, they are more likely to deny their naturally occurring feelings or suppress instead of express those feelings, and possibly end up lost in the wilderness of complicated grief.

- Grief and mourning proceed in predictable, orderly stages.
- You should move away from grief, not toward it.
- Tears and other demonstrative behaviors in grief are signs of weakness, especially for men.
- Openly mourning means you are being weak in your faith.
- It's best to "get over" your grief as quickly as possible.

- Nobody can help you with your grief; it's something you have to come to terms with yourself.

- Grief that lasts a long time is abnormal.

- The person who died wouldn't want you to be sad.

Such misconceptions are essentially fake maps of the wilderness of grief. "Go this way," they promise. "This is the fastest, easiest route." If you've ever had Siri or Google Maps blithely lead you to the wrong destination, you understand the trouble that ill-conceived maps can get us into.

And fourth, our culture has increasingly moved toward the **deritualization of loss and death**. When everyday words and actions are inadequate, as is the case when a loved one dies, ceremony is essential to helping us embark on a solid path in the wilderness—one that leads to healing. But we are abandoning our religious and social communities that uphold ritual, our funerals are getting shorter, and with the trend toward memorial services, we are separated from both the time of the death and the body of the person who died. We're having parties instead of gatherings that help us embrace and express our necessary sadness and support one another. And it's becoming more and more common for ceremony to be skipped altogether.

When you add all of these cultural influences up, what you have is an environment in which grief is likely to be denied, suppressed, and/or unsupported. In such circumstances, it's not a stretch to see that normal grief can easily become complicated grief—even in cases in which none of the other influences in this section definitely apply.

In recent years, I have been heartened to see more open public conversations about the normalcy of grief. The popularity of the recent book by Facebook Chief Operating Officer Sheryl Sandberg about the unexpected death of her husband, *Option B*, is just one example of this cultural shift. I am hopeful that one day in the not-too-distant future the principles of grief will be reviewed and openly discussed in schools, and that future generations will grow up knowing that grief and mourning are as normal and necessary as love, healthy relationships, and good interpersonal skills. I also hope death and funerals return to being more normalized, essential, personal, and meaningful rites of passage.

> "I'd always been told that if you want something done right, do it yourself. So, after the sudden death of my husband, I kept to myself and actually pushed people away. It wasn't until I went into a major depression and had to get help that I discovered I couldn't do this alone. After that I started to get the support I needed, and being able to do that and get some good counseling has really saved my life."

In the meantime, though, be on the lookout for insidious societal contributors to complicated grief as you companion struggling grievers. When the time is right, many complicated grievers need help seeing the cultural influences on their grief experiences as well as permission to forge for themselves a new, better path.

2. CIRCUMSTANCES OF THE DEATH

When we love someone and they die, we suffer grief. As I have noted, grief is always challenging and complicated. But certain loss circumstances tend to be exceptionally and understandably challenging and complicated, making the experience of complicated grief more likely.

Sudden, unexpected death

Even when someone we love is terminally ill and death is imminent, I have observed that we are never really ready for the death. The transition from "alive" to "dead" always comes as a shock. There is simply no preparing for lifelessness in a body that had animated a soul we cared deeply about. But when a death is sudden and unexpected, feelings of shock and unreality are compounded. Accidental deaths fall into this category, as do military deaths, murders, suicides, and deaths by sudden illness.

In such cases, a heightened sense of unreality is common, as is a focus on the particulars and day of the death. For these and all the death circumstances we will be discussing in the following paragraphs, an extended period of shock and numbness is common.

Sometimes insensitive or inappropriate death notification also plays a role in the grief that follows sudden, unexpected deaths. Medical and law enforcement staff, for example, are not always empathetic communicators. In addition, the immediacy and informality of social media and texting sometimes result in next of kin first hearing about a death in unsuitable ways. "I just heard your son was the person in that fatal car accident! I'm so sorry!" someone might post on Facebook—before the parent even knew there had been a car accident.

It's also normal for grievers to be traumatized by certain death circumstances, especially those that in addition to being sudden and unexpected are also violent. In an effort to understand and come to terms with what has happened, the human mind tends to replay or reimagine the event of the violent death over and over. In this way, complicated grief and post-traumatic stress may overlap. People affected by traumatic deaths have special needs, and we will discuss how to help them meet these needs in Part Three. And always remember that each griever will teach you whether or not he considers the death he is mourning "traumatic." In the ways that matter most, this is a subjective categorization. What truly counts is the griever's experience and inner reality.

> "Throughout my childhood, I was physically and emotionally abused by my father. I'm in college now, and my father recently killed himself, and I was the one who discovered the body. I'm really depressed and have been considering suicide."

Before-time death

The death of a young person is always hard to accept. Especially now, in the age of modern medicine, we can be reasonably confident that the young people we love will have the opportunity to grow to adulthood. But though the odds are in our favor, there are no such guarantees, of course. Children still die of disease, accidents, and homicide. Some tragically die by suicide.

Keep in mind that our sense that a death has occurred before its time extends to young adults and even middle-aged friends and family members. As longevity increases, we simply expect people to live longer. Today, we take it for granted that most people will live into their 80s or 90s. So when a 64-year-old dies, for example, we might well consider that this person died "before his time"— especially if we ourselves are middle-aged or older than the person who died.

In addition to a prolonged period of shock and numbness, people grieving an early death may be more likely to experience more pronounced feelings of guilt and explosive emotions, which are a form of protest.

I also consider it a before-time death when a parent of a child dies.

From the child's point of view, the parent has broken a contract of sorts. By a young age, children tacitly understand that parents or parent figures are supposed to take care of them at least until they grow to adulthood. When this promise is broken by premature death, the child naturally struggles to come to terms with the foundational collapse in his life. For many young people it can seem like the laws of physics have been violated. It feels disorienting, scary, frustrating, and unjust.

Out-of-order death

When someone dies whom we believe should have outlived us, we sense that the death is out of order. It's as if a rule of nature has been broken. Whenever a child dies before a parent or grandparent, for example, this is the case—even when the child is an adult.

As with a before-time death, in addition to an extended period of shock and numbness, people grieving an out-of-order death may experience more pronounced feelings of guilt and explosive emotions. Guilt often arises when people perceive they have unfairly outlived or failed to protect a younger person. Anger and other explosive emotions protest the injustice of a life cut short.

Means of death

Certain types of deaths make them naturally more challenging for grievers to acknowledge and encounter the pain. These include deaths by suicide, homicide, and senseless accidents, of course, but also military deaths, terrorism deaths, deaths by natural disasters, and others. We find them incomprehensible.

In general, the more violent and extreme the circumstances of the death, the harder it is for grievers to move beyond shock and numbness, acknowledge the reality of the death, and embrace the pain of the loss. The same can be said of random deaths and deaths that are perceived as having been preventable. Any social stigmas commonly associated with some of these types of death, such as suicide and deaths caused by what may be perceived as bad judgment or foolhardy risk-taking, further compound the complications.

Because they are intentional and premature, among other reasons, suicide and homicide are especially naturally complicating death circumstances, each with their own unique and profound challenges.

The terrain of suicide grief is always harrowing. It is unfathomable that someone you love, cherish, and maybe depend on would physically and permanently remove herself from this world and from you *on purpose.* This breaks the contract of love. This flouts the sanctity of life. Prolonged shock and numbness are common, of course, as is the need to try to understand the un-understandable. It's normal to search for "why" and new meaning in life, but when meaning rules have been broken by suicide, the search is often both all-consuming and endless. Self-blame, blame directed at others (including the person who died), and anger are typical though not always present. Meanwhile, autopsies, police investigations, media coverage, and life insurance issues create more strife and pain and may cause secondary victimization. And the means of death is often a naturally traumatic focus for survivors, especially those who witnessed the death or discovered the body of the person who died.

Homicide grief has similar features, although much of the griever's emotional and spiritual energy is often directed at the person who caused the death. In addition, homicides are typically violent, and grievers naturally and understandably struggle to come to terms with the death experience of the person who died. The brutal nature of the death often engenders the fear response of traumatic stress. And the criminal investigation, prosecution, and media demands of homicide deaths can consume the energies of loved ones for years, essentially delaying healthy grief and mourning. When the court battles finally wrap up, these families don't really have closure; in some ways their grief journeys are really just beginning.

Deaths by opioid overdose, which are now epidemic in the United States, result in similar challenges for grievers. Like deaths by suicide and homicide, overdose deaths are stigmatized in our culture, so grievers typically struggle with both lack of support and intense shame, anger, and guilt. Grievers are often angry at the person who died, at others whom they perceive enabled the behavior (such as a drug dealer), and/or at medical staff or police who may have been involved. Guilt and feelings of helplessness commonly arise over grievers' inability to have prevented the drug use and death, even though the behavior was outside their control.

Finally, deaths after a lengthy illness may also complicate the terrain of grief. While these deaths are usually very different from deaths caused by suicide or homicide, they can also be harrowing. Grievers who witnessed extended declines caused by some cancers or dementia and who may have been a primary caregiver, for example, come to grief after a long period of stress and often naturally heightened dependence. The stress may have been financial as well as physical, cognitive, emotional, social, and spiritual. Bioethical challenges may have come into play, in which grievers had to make difficult decisions about life-prolonging care or uncertain treatments. Anger and guilt are common, as are numbness and a sense of loss of meaning.

Uncertainty surrounding the death

Whenever there is uncertainty about how a death occurred, our grief is likely to be more complicated. Our minds and hearts yearn to understand. Sometimes the uncertainty is the result of unknown, confusing, or withheld circumstances or details, and sometimes the body goes missing or cannot be recovered and autopsied.

I often say that we can cope with what we know, but it is extremely challenging to cope with what we don't know. Grievers who must learn to cope with unknowable circumstances, especially if they were unable to view the body or visit the site of the death, have special needs that companions can help them meet with the use of techniques reviewed in Part Three.

> "My 22-year-old son died after jumping in front of an
> oncoming train. Because of the nature of his injuries, I didn't
> ask to view his body. The option wasn't offered to me, either.
> It has been two years since he died and I am still struggling
> with acknowledging the reality of his death. It feels like he just
> vanished from my life."

Physical distance from the death

When someone we love is far away from us when they die, we tend to feel a sense of impeded separation. Time and distance are in our way. We often feel the need to be close to the body and to see for ourselves the place and the circumstances of the death. Sometimes we are not aware of these needs right away, and by the time we are aware of them, it is too late. At other times, we are simply unable to travel to the place of the death.

For grievers who were separated from the person who died, especially if they were never able to view the body, the death may seem unreal. For example, a 21-year-old young woman traveled to the Caribbean for spring break and ended up drowning there. Her body was not recovered. Years later, her parents told me that they still keep waiting for her to walk through the door. As with many of the loss circumstances we are discussing in this section, the heightened sense of unreality often stalls movement in the grief journey. You can help restart it.

Self-blame for the death

If we feel at fault in any way for a death, our sense of guilt, regret, or shame will of course impact our grief. Oftentimes we are not actually guilty of any wrongdoing, but we still need to explore our self-blame in order to move beyond it.

One example of this is when family members must make the painful decision to remove a loved one from life support. Such measures are only taken after much agonizing and thoughtful counsel by medical providers, but still, it is common and understandable for family decision-makers to continue to question whether or not they did the right thing.

Grievers who blame themselves for some aspect of the death or for circumstances that led up to the death need help exploring these feelings. Our job as companions is not to take away their guilt but rather to create safe ways for them to encounter it.

3. THE GRIEVER'S UNIQUE PERSONALITY

Each of us has our own unique ways of being in the world. Some of these predilections and habits come about through interactions with our families of origin, and some are inborn traits. Still others we develop as we mature and go through life.

Of course, you have probably had exposure to the various theories of personality in your training. From Freud and Skinner to Maslow and Rogers, a number of marquee mental-health clinicians have proffered models for understanding the genesis, development, and analysis of individuals' personalities. I won't go into those models here, but your knowledge of them may help you in your work with grievers.

For purposes of this discussion, I am casting a wide net and also including a number of tangential variables under the heading "personality," including capacity to access emotionality, mental health, addiction, ability to care for self, and relationship histories.

Extroversion/introversion

We have said that grief is internal and mourning is external. We have also said that mourning is essential to healing. Very generally speaking, we may assume that introverts may have a harder time mourning, including reaching out to others, while extroverts may struggle more with acknowledging and befriending the inward work of grief.

Emotionality

Emotionality is the griever's capacity to feel, embrace, and express his emotions. While there is no single right way to do this, grievers who tend to avoid or suppress emotion, intellectualize or control emotion, or express emotions in distorted ways often experience complicated grief. Those who are mentored or surrounded by people who promote the misconception that emotionality is bad also often struggle. What's more, in loss circumstances that are particularly challenging, grievers who are normally adept at healthy emotionality may find themselves overwhelmed.

Keep in mind, however, that not everyone mourns through the expression of deep emotion. People grieve and mourn differently, and a lack of a labile or dramatic affect does not mean that any given griever is not doing the work he needs to do. It is vital for grief companions to be respectful of each mourner's unique emotionality and grieving style. Some people have never been demonstrative with their feelings, particularly those of affection and loss. These people will naturally be more reserved in their mourning. At the same time, however, it is important for grief companions to help reserved mourners feel safe enough to express feelings that they might normally hide. In my experience, reserved grievers do feel deeply inside and are coming to you for help in connecting with and expressing their emotional selves.

A retired professor was once referred to me for grief counseling by a local hospice. His wife of many years had died several months before. In our first session, the first words out of his mouth to me were, "What will be the intensity and duration of this experience?" I quickly learned that he was someone who tried to intellectualize and problem solve. In other words, he was attempting to think his way through grief, and it wasn't working. After we had established a relationship of mutual respect and trust, toward the close of each session I asked him to read a piece of his wife's poetry aloud to me. Her poems seemed to bypass his brain and directly touch his tender heart. As he read, he cried. And as he cried, he slowly, week by week, began to integrate her death into his continuing life. Now, not everyone is a crier, but had we not found a way for him to access his profound emotions—which were there all along, of course—he would not have been able to reconcile his grief as deeply as he eventually did.

As psychotherapist David Richo wrote, "A yes to feelings is the station stop before we get to philosophical explanations, theological consolations, or encouraging maxims."

Mental health

Any current or past mental-health challenges grievers may have will naturally have an impact on their grief experience. Those with a history of depression or anxiety, for example, are at risk for deepened depression and heightened anxiety in grief, especially in traumatic loss circumstances. Since both depression and anxiety are normal symptoms of grief, however, it is incumbent on the companion to keep a close eye on these features in mourners with such histories and consider medical treatment in addition to grief companioning when appropriate. As with all aspects of grief, gray areas abound, and each mourner needs and deserves highly personalized attention and care. Of course, grievers with dementia or other special needs also merit special care. (A brochure for families and caregivers I authored entitled "Helping a Person with Alzheimer's or Memory Loss Understand News of a Death" is available at www.centerforloss.com.)

Physical health

Injury, disability, and illness, whether chronic or acute, can also be risk factors for complicated grief. First, physical health problems are often stressful, compounding the natural stress of grief. And second, sometimes the person who died was involved in helping care for the griever and his health challenges, leaving the griever at loose ends. Until and unless the griever's physical health can be stabilized, it may be impossible for her to devote adequate time and energy to mourning and healing.

Addiction

The science of addiction is still emerging, but we believe that addiction may have genetic components in addition to its social and behavioral influences. For purposes of this discussion, it is sufficient to say that grievers who have struggled with addiction in the past are at heightened risk of addictive behaviors during their grief journeys, especially when the grief is already complicated. And conversely, normal grief, when combined with addiction, can easily escalate into complicated grief, especially when you consider the sequelae of addiction, which include health consequences, relationship issues, financial disaster, etc.

Addicts typically find temporary refuge and symptoms relief in their habit, whether that habit involves drugs, alcohol, gambling, shopping, sex, or any other substance or behavior. Grief is so naturally hurtful that it is understandable when people turn to their addictions to alleviate the pain, even though doing so arrests the capacity to actively mourn. In fact, addictive behaviors in grief have been my most frequent referral over the years. As grief companion, you are responsible to help keep the griever safe and on a healthy mourning path. Learning about addiction history and being watchful for current addictive patterns are essential parts of your work.

"During the tough times in my life, I always seemed to turn to alcohol. When my son died from brain cancer, I picked up my drinking even more— went from beer to straight vodka. It didn't take long until my wife pointed out that I was self-treating my pain and was totally in my own little world—and she wasn't part of it. I later learned that I was trying to mourn but couldn't until I got help for my drinking. Then and only then could I really mourn in ways that helped me start some healing from the death of my wonderful son."

Generally speaking, I have found that addicts need addiction treatment before they can benefit from grief counseling. Only when they are in active recovery are they in a position to focus on their grief and benefit from companion-fostered mourning. Even though grief and loss may be root causes of their current addiction struggles, the ongoing use of their drug of choice is an insurmountable barrier to effective mourning. Once they have achieved and committed to sobriety, however, and continue to receive addiction support as needed, they are ready to engage with their grief and mourning. It's a question of sequence, and a case in which getting the sequence out of order yields little or no benefits for the suffering griever.

Ability to care for self
Mental-health professionals are accustomed to assessing their clients for self-care habits, including the basic activities of daily

living, such as eating, sleeping, nutrition, hygiene, dressing, and exercise. When I inquired about self-care with one new client, she shared that she ate ice cream three times a day. People who are unable to step through the activities of daily living are considered to be in need of immediate and intensive care. More broadly, self-care activities include sufficiently attending to ones own physical, cognitive, emotional, social, sexual, financial, and spiritual needs. People with a serious deficit in any of these areas before they came to grief are simply more at risk for complicated grief.

History of conflicted or abusive relationships

We'll talk about the griever's relationship with the person who died next, but setting aside that particular relationship for the moment, I have noticed that people who have a history of ambivalent or abusive relationships are more vulnerable in general to complicated grief. Why? Remember that grief is essentially a form of love, or attachment. Those who have experienced unhealthy attachments—whether through their own doing, the other party's doing, or a combination of the two—are more likely to also experience unhealthy grief patterns, which is complicated grief. As you companion grievers with a history of conflicted or abusive relationships, you may discern that their often-unconscious assumptions and unwritten rules about emotionality, self-care, and relationship dynamics contribute to their complicated grief and serve as barriers to healing.

4. THE GRIEVER'S RELATIONSHIP WITH THE
   PERSON WHO DIED

People are unique, and so are their relationships. It is wise for you as grief companion to keep that in mind each time you meet a new griever. In fact, the more you can empty your mind of preconceptions and adopt a clean-slate, "teach-me" attitude, the more helpful you will be.

When one member in certain types of relationships dies, the surviving member may be more likely to develop complicated grief. For example, when a child dies, the parents are at risk of complicated grief because the parent-child relationship is usually so very close and interdependent. The same goes for soulmates. (You may find it helpful to use my book *When Your Soulmate Dies* as an educational resource and guided journaling text for grieving soulmates.) But someone who is grieving the loss of a friend, sibling, grandparent, colleague, or elderly parent may also develop complicated grief. In fact, sometimes complicated grief arises in the most unlikely-seeming of relationships. That is why it is essential to jettison preconceptions and ask each griever to teach you about their unique relationship.

In general, though, there are two measures of relationship that can help you discern who may be at risk for complicated grief—strength of attachment and complexity of attachment. The stronger the griever's attachment to the person who died, typically the more challenging and painful the grief journey may be. Also, the more complex the attachment, such as in conflicted or abusive relationships, the more complicated the grief journey may be.

Beyond this general guidance, here are a few relationship dynamics to be on the watch for:

Extreme dependence
Grievers who were exceptionally dependent on or interdependent with the person who died are at high risk of complicated grief. This dependence can take many forms. Often the griever's self-identity was tightly intertwined with that of the person who died. We see this in longtime partners (who often married or partnered young and, in our couple-oriented culture, may lack individual identities outside the relationship), parents who have lost a child, twins, and even adult children who have lived with or cared for aging or ill

parents. It makes sense, and it is a perfectly normal consequence of having been powerfully attached to another human being. It's common for these grievers to say, "I feel like I died too" or "A big part of me died that day." In addition, any time the griever realized a strong sense of meaning and purpose in life from the relationship, the grief is likely to be complicated once the relationship is ended by death. The natural dependence of children and young adults on a parent also falls into this category, as does financial dependence.

I once counseled the family of an ex-postman who had died suddenly of a heart attack. The man and his wife had been extremely close for many years, especially after his early retirement due to a disability. They spent every moment of every day together. Shortly after his death, the couple's two adult daughters both separated from their husbands to move back home with their mother. During family therapy with the daughters and the mother, I learned that the daughters unconsciously felt compelled to replace their father's companionship of their mother with theirs because if they did not, their mother, too, would die. I supported the mother through her complicated grief, helping her be self-responsible for her journey through the wilderness. I helped the daughters understand and engage with their complicated grief as well as establish healthy boundaries. The daughters returned to their own homes, and the mother continued to work on mourning and reconciling her grief.

Unreconciled conflict or ambivalence

While some relationships are close and loving, others are close and conflicted, and still others are on-again/off-again, love-hate, or estranged altogether. All can result in complicated grief in the griever. Unreconciled relationship issues, or "unfinished business," can be particularly hard for grievers to navigate, as time has run out. Often people in precarious relationships hope and expect that one day things will be resolved, but when death intervenes, that day can never come. You may notice, as I have, that the grief is often as complicated as the attachment in such circumstances.

> "My 40-year-old adopted daughter suddenly collapsed and died. She had struggled with mental illness and addiction for many years, and her extreme behavioral issues made our life together really challenging. After her death, her daughter—my granddaughter—tried to kill herself. I feel so guilty."

History of abuse, addiction, or mental illness

We've already discussed what can happen to grief when the griever has a personal history of abuse, addiction, or mental illness. When the person who died has any of these histories, the same thinking applies. They simply complicate relationships, and when the relationship is complicated, the resulting grief is complicated. Even if the person who died might not have been considered mentally ill or abusive but was difficult, controlling, or distant, complicated grief may follow. In these situations, the griever's grief typically includes not only natural sadness but also anger, regret, relief, and other complex combinations. A history of abuse within the relationship between the griever and the person who died is also complicating, of course, and merits gentle, compassionate exploration.

> "My partner of 40 years died. She was a paraplegic, and I took care of her. People thought she was my aunt. It's difficult to come out of the closet simply because your soulmate has died. You can't cope with your grief without laying on top of that coming out. And when someone you were caring for dies, you lose your job and your purpose in life. You become redundant as well as bereft."

WHEN GRIEF IS COMPLICATED

Disenfranchised relationships

Grievers who shared a disenfranchised relationship with the person who died are at risk of complicated grief. Social recognition and support is one of the central needs of mourning (see pg. 147), but it is often not available to survivors of relationships that were not recognized and supported in the first place. This sometimes applies to stigmatized relationships, such as same-sex couples, as well as secretive relationships and relationships that tend to be minimized by our culture, such as those between adult siblings.

Secondary losses as part of complicated grief

Whenever someone dies, grievers don't just experience the loss of the physical presence of the person. They also suffer a variety of tangential losses. This tends to be especially true in complicated grief, because the more complicated the loss circumstances, the more complicated the terrain, and the more complicated the terrain, the more facets of the griever's life are impacted by the challenge. As companion, you have an obligation to be respectful of the multitude of ripple-effect losses that often impact the complicated griever. Here are some common examples.

Loss of self

- *self*—"I feel like part of me died when he died."

- *identity*—Mourners often have to rethink roles as husband or wife, mother or father, son or daughter, best friend, etc.

- *self-confidence*—Some grievers experience lowered self-esteem. Naturally, mourners may have lost one of the people in their lives who gave them confidence.

- *health*—Physical symptoms of mourning

- *personality*—"I just don't feel like myself..."

Loss of security

- *emotional security*—Emotional source of support is now gone, causing emotional upheaval.

- *physical security*—Mourners may not feel as safe living in their homes or communities as they did before.

- *fiscal security*—Mourners may have financial concerns or have to learn to manage finances in ways they didn't before.

- *lifestyle*—The mourner's lifestyle doesn't feel the same as it did before.

Loss of meaning

- *goals and dreams*—Hopes and dreams for the future can be shattered.

- *faith*—Mourners often question their faith.

- *will/desire to live*—Mourners often have questions related to future meaning in their lives. They may ask, "Why go on...?"

- *joy*—Life's most precious emotion, happiness, is naturally compromised by the death of someone we love.

What other secondary losses have you born witness to in your work with complicated grievers? How have you helped these grievers acknowledge and mourn the many ripple effects of their loss?

5. THE GRIEVER'S LOSS HISTORY

Human life is replete with attachment and thus loss.

Simply, we're made to love and connect. It's built into our DNA From the moment we're born, we begin to form attachments to people, animals, places, things, and experiences. Whenever strong attachments are severed or compromised—through death, divorce, illness, relocation, or changing circumstances—we feel a sense of loss, and we naturally grieve inside.

As we grow, we learn to accommodate our grief. Our parents and other significant adults in our lives model the experience of grief and mourning, typically in both healthy and unhealthy ways. Our culture, which we've already discussed, provides strong and often stultifying cues. Our schools and our peers also influence what is "appropriate" and what is not. And we ourselves, shaped by our unique personalities, our developmental stages, as well as all of these additional influences, experiment and learn ways to keep putting one foot in front of another, despite our losses.

In other words, grief doesn't really emerge anew after each new loss. Instead, each new grief experience is built upon all former grief experiences. After all, it's the same with love. We find our way through new relationships based on understanding we have gleaned from longer-term or past relationships. In both cases— love and grief—we've developed habits, fears, likes, dislikes. Our propensities, which may meander over time but typically remain tethered in recognizable ways to our histories, determine our behavior.

Therefore, the complicated grievers who come to you for support have a loss history that is just as salient and important as a patient's medical history is to a physician. They are experiencing complicated grief in the present, yes, but their current complicated grief is always, at least to some degree, affected by their loss, grief, and mourning experiences in the past.

The past losses can bring to the present experience a preexisting sense of personal vulnerability in the griever. Whenever we as humans feel torn apart, we can experience a sense of loss of control. And this loss of control often activates feelings of helplessness, hurt, pain, and fear. Significant present loss often retriggers feelings of anxiety and vulnerability. This retriggering can impact one's sense of overall safety and security.

"When I was 14 my mom died from breast cancer. I was the oldest of three children, and everyone said I needed to be strong and take care of my dad and my two little brothers. They kept saying you are the woman of the house. So, I stuffed my grief and went about my business. Then, when I was 39 my dad died and my entire world fell apart. With the help of a good grief therapist I discovered I needed not only to mourn my dad's death but go backward and finally mourn my mom. I learned I had to go backward to be able to go forward."

As a therapist, you must be able to recognize when the griever's previous losses (death as well as other significant life transitions) are creeping into or impacting the current loss. While this is a normal phenomenon that occurs, the complication is that you often have to give attention to the prior loss before the griever is able to give attention to the current loss.

I often frame this for myself as a sequence issue. I have seen caregivers attempt to focus on the present loss to the exclusion of the previous loss, and it simply doesn't work. Grievers who shine the light on prior losses are trying to teach me. They are in effect saying, "I need you to help me go backward to the prior loss before I can go forward to the present loss. Can you help me do that?" This is a great reminder that when it comes to complicated grief, you will get many invitations to go backward with the griever before you can forward. A common error made by some caregivers is attempting to focus on the present loss and push the griever forward.

All of this can be true of normal grief, of course. We are all products of our past. But for complicated grievers, their pasts often (but not always) include loss, grief, and mourning experiences that were also complicated and unreconciled. To use the vernacular, they have "baggage" having to do with loss and grief. In fact, I describe them as "carrying grief."

What is **carried grief**? Carried grief is accumulated grief from life losses that have never been adequately acknowledged and mourned. What may appear to be complicated grief due to a recent loss is often more aptly characterized as pent-up, burgeoning grief from a lifetime of losses. The latest loss may have been especially challenging in various ways, and thus a candidate for complicated grief all on its own, or it may on the surface seem commonplace or relatively insignificant. Either way—but especially the latter— carried grief must be considered as part of the source.

As you companion a complicated griever, you will, over time, be learning her story. In piecing together the puzzle of her life, you may well come to realize that, for a variety of reasons, the griever carries unexplored and unreconciled grief from other deaths and significant losses as well. It stands to reason that tendencies to avoid, distort, or minimize grief in the past would continue into the present, yet the griever is often unaware that her current challenges and frustrating patterns may have been long in the making.

In Part Two we will be looking at common symptoms of carried grief. For now it suffices to say that companions must always be on the lookout for carried grief. This topic is so important that some years ago I wrote a book about it for grievers themselves entitled

Living in the Shadow of the Ghosts of Grief: Step Into the Light. You may find it a helpful addition to your professional library, and if you are companioning mourners through reconciling carried grief, it may be a good resource for them as well because it will help them develop insight into their challenges.

6. THE GRIEVER'S ACCESS TO AND USE OF SUPPORT

Healthy mourning requires the ongoing support of other human beings. Healing requires an environment of empathy, caring, and gentle encouragement. Grievers who lack such support or mistakenly believe they don't need it are thwarted in their journey to healing.

Does the griever have close friends and family members who provide assistance and regular contact? Is the griever engaged in social, community, and/or spiritual groups? Does the griever have at least one other reliable, compassionate person to spend time with and open up to? Has support continued beyond the first month or two after the death? Unless the answer to all four questions is "yes," the griever's support may be insufficient, increasing the likelihood of complicated grief. Grievers whose only source of love and support was the person who died are particularly at risk.

"I was the first among our friends to experience the death of my spouse. We had been very close to three other couples. After Don died they came to the funeral, but then they all seemed to just go away. It was like they were afraid it was going to happen to them. I was shocked and really depressed about how I felt abandoned by them. I ended up having to create new friends, some of whom had also experienced the death of their spouses. That helped me feel safe and gave me the courage to go see a counselor and mourn in ways I needed."

Of course, the availability of support is only half the equation. Accepting support is the other half. Not all grievers are equipped with the emotionality, healthy vulnerability, and interpersonal skills it takes to make good use of the offered empathy and support of others. Some simply do not make the time, while others are in special circumstances that make it all but impossible for them to accept support. This may happen if a griever is hospitalized or living far from their friends and family, for instance. What's more, many grievers (as well as their friends and family members) have, through no fault of their own, been contaminated by our culture's misconception that nobody can help you with your grief and that you just have to keep your chin up and get on with life.

As I listen to each griever's support story, I am always on the watch for answers to these three questions:

1. Does the griever have a support system? Not all do.

2. Do the supporters the griever describes encourage open, authentic mourning? Some would-be supporters are in fact grief deniers or, worse yet, grief shamers.

3. Does the griever have the capacity to search out and make use of support? Some grievers are help rejecters.

As you work with grievers, be on the watch for those who are isolated and/or incapable of accepting support. Their grief will probably be complicated, and your helping relationship with them will be especially important.

7. OTHER CONCURRENT STRESSORS IN THE GRIEVER'S LIFE

Part of the reason that grief is always complicated is that life is always complicated. There are a lot of moving parts—health, education, aging, relationships, children, parents, finances, job, social connections, spiritual affiliations, and more—not to mention births and deaths. People in grief often remark that even though someone who gave their life meaning died, life does not stand still. All of the obligations I listed continue on, ceaselessly and relentlessly.

When an elderly parent dies, for example, a griever may experience normal, uncomplicated grief. But when that same parent dies during a time period in which the griever is undergoing divorce, changing jobs, dealing with dysfunctional family dynamics, battling health problems, or struggling with any other significant losses or challenges, **loss overload** often compounds and complicates grief. The griever may be equipped to effectively navigate any one or two of these circumstances, but too many too close together would overwhelm anyone. Again, in such cases, complicated grief is simply a normal response to an abnormally extreme situation.

I often use the analogy of a pressure cooker to describe grief circumstances in which there is a lot of stress and not enough support or coping strategies to go around. This happens when a griever experiences lots of different stresses at the same time. It may also occur when multiple people in the same family or household are affected by a loss as well as other concurrent demands. Add pressure, and the pressure cooker starts to pressurize.

Sometimes the concurrent stressors are multiple deaths within a relatively short period of time. When several loved ones die, there's no time to acknowledge, embrace, and express one grief before the next one arrives uninvited. This is another form of **loss overload**, and it's a common cause of complicated grief. Sometimes grievers experience serial losses—one death followed by another and then another in a relatively short period of time—and sometimes grievers suffer the loss of more than one person in the same incident, such as a car crash. Regardless of the type of loss overload, companioning grievers through it often simply requires providing them with a safe, compassionate environment for decompressing, storying, and expressing pent-up emotions. I always adjust my expectations with loss overload as it will go very slowly. Each loss requires separate attention. You can't put them all together.

> "During the years when I was 17 to 20, my best friend, my boyfriend, my brother, both of my grandfathers, and my father all died. Also, shortly after the last death I moved overseas with my husband, who was in the military. I tried to process all my losses alone and thought I was going crazy. I really wanted to die. I yearned so hard for my brother that I felt I couldn't breathe, but then I would feel guilt for the many others I had lost also. I began to drink, party all night, and fight with my husband. My wild behavior went on for six years. I was out of control. I'm lucky to be alive."

Whether they are secondary losses that directly stem from the primary loss or concurrent but technically unrelated challenges, other significant changes during a time of intense grief can have the same effect. Job loss, relocation, life-altering or life-threatening health challenges, financial upsets, family upheavals such as discord, unintended pregnancy, or addiction—any such turmoil during a time of intense grief understandably compounds stress, distracts from mourning, and delays healing.

> "After my husband's sudden death from a debilitating illness, I had to take over the family business. I also had to mother my two grieving young adult children. I had no time to process or

express my grief. My mask was on. I didn't consciously think of it as a mask at that time, but my body was protecting me from going to a place that would be far too painfully overwhelming to handle."

Complicated grievers impacted by multiple concurrent stressors often need reassurance that their circumstances would overtax anyone's capacity to cope. They may also need referral to a network of community resources for help with various issues. In the case of loss overload, the griever may simply need support more frequently and for a longer period of time. I have also found that loss-overloaded grievers often feel overwhelmed and need more guidance about how to approach their multiple losses. Understandably, they don't know where to start. You can help by encouraging them to focus on one loss at a time or creating a mourning plan or structure that feels safe and doable to them.

8. THE GRIEVER'S CULTURAL/ETHNIC BACKGROUND

Our cultural and/or ethnic background is an important part of how we experience and express our grief. When I say culture, I mean the values, rules (spoken and unspoken), and traditions that have been handed down generation after generation and are often shaped by the countries or areas of the world we originally came from. Educational and political beliefs are also aspects of our cultural background. Basically, our culture is our way of being in the world.

We've already talked about our society's lack of understanding of and respect for grief and pain. That affects all of us. Here I want you to consider the unique cultural or ethnic influences that each individual griever may be affected by. People raised in a Japanese-American household will probably have different norms and traditions than people whose ancestors are from Mexico, for example. Not only are their funeral ceremonies and customs different, but their understanding of death and grief may be fundamentally different.

> "I think my German heritage kinda taught me to keep a stiff upper lip. After my wife died many people told me I needed to cry. I have never been one to cry, and I'm 76 years old. I figured, why should I start now! So I had to find some other ways to mourn. I chopped lots of wood and found one other man in the same situation. He and I still meet for coffee three times a week."

In Ireland and Scotland, for example, it is customary for women grievers to loudly wail, or keen, during the funeral procession and at the burial site. They may also combine their vocalizations with physical movement such as rocking or clapping. Keening is an unapologetically public and ritualized expression of inner grief. As such, it is a practice that helps grievers mourn at a time when everyday words and actions are inadequate.

When it comes to complicated grief, you may need to dig deeper to understand any cultural or ethnic influences that may be contributing. The question is not so much what any culture or ethnicity dictates; the question is what this unique griever finds important, meaningful, or possibly unhelpful when it comes to his culture's grief norms.

9. THE GRIEVER'S RELIGIOUS/SPIRITUAL/ PHILOSOPHICAL BACKGROUND

Our belief systems can have a tremendous impact on our grief. After all, death is typically considered the purview of religion or spirituality. Bodies of faith often dictate customs to follow after a death and teach us how we are supposed to feel about death.

While faith gives many grievers great solace, some grievers end up suppressing their normal and necessary grief because their body of faith teaches that mourning and faith are mutually exclusive. In other words, they should not mourn because their loved one is in a better place. Instead, they should rejoice. Mourning may be equated with weakness or lack of faith.

I was once contacted by a woman who had suffered two stillbirths. Her clergyperson had been counseling her through her grief for a couple of years before she came to me. Unfortunately, the woman's grief had been rendered more complicated by this counseling experience because the clergyperson had repeatedly suggested to her that her ongoing anxiety and depression were signs that she was being weak in her faith. Of course, this non-supportive stance only served to heighten her anxiety and depression. Fortunately, I was able to connect her with a Center for Loss graduate who had earned our certification in death and grief studies, which included training in complicated grief. This therapist companioned her using the principles described in Part Three of this book, and she was eventually able to integrate her naturally complicated grief over the loss of her precious children and find her way to hope and healing.

In addition, a body of faith's mourning rules and customs sometimes aren't what a griever feels naturally inclined to follow. If she goes her own way, she may be judged as sinful or heretical. For example, some grievers take up new spiritual practices to help them mourn, such as meditation or spending time in nature in lieu of attending services, and may be shamed for doing so. What's more, some grievers are separated from their body of faith, either through distance or attrition.

Religious messages that may inhibit and complicate mourning

Grievers are often offered religious platitudes in lieu of truly empathetic support. Note that even religious grievers may feel offended or shut down by such messages because what they really need is a chance to express how they're feeling and receive unconditional support, and clichés tend to forestall real conversation and care. Here are some of the more common ones. I'm sure you can think of others.

• God wouldn't give you more than you can handle.

• She's watching over you.

• God has a plan for you.

• He's in a better place.

• It's a test of your faith.

• Everything happens for a reason.

• This is all part of God's plan.

• God works in mysterious ways.

• This happened to bring you to God.

• God needed a special angel.

• I'm praying for you.

Prayer, by the way, is welcomed by many grievers but may also be seen as insufficient. "I'm praying for you" is not the same as "I'm here to help you and listen to you," and grievers often feel abandoned or left in the lurch. Nonreligious grievers may feel outright disrespected when they are repeatedly told, "I am praying for you."

Grievers who are significantly conflicted about their faith and their grief and mourning will experience this as a complication in their grief journey. You will need them to teach you about what this experience is like for them, and they will need you to listen, bear witness, encourage, and be a sounding board for any problem-solving ideas they may have.

10. THE GRIEVER'S FAMILY SYSTEMS INFLUENCES

Each of us is born into a family from whom we learn rules, spoken and unspoken, about values, behaviors, social norms, emotionality, and spirituality. We carry these rules into our adult lives, and we are often unaware of how deeply embedded they are in our every feeling and response.

Grievers raised in a closed family system often lack healthy self-awareness, emotionality, and communication skills. They may have been taught that death and grief are inappropriate to discuss, let alone express feelings about, and that it's best just to "get over it" and "move on." They may also believe that seeking the help of a counselor means admitting "weakness." Such conditions make complicated grief more likely.

Of course, family systems influences in grief do not only stem from the griever's family of origin. The griever's current family, which may include close and influential friends, will also have a significant effect on her grief response. A lack of current close family or family surrogates—or family members separated by distance—is also a complicater.

In addition, some complicated grievers may be, in effect, dealing with multigenerational carried grief. In a closed family system, the suicide of a great-grandmother may have never been fully acknowledged or mourned by her spouse and thus her children, who then taught their children that death and grief are taboo, and so on. Unhealthy family rules around emotionality often affect many people for generations.

In the 1970s, the American psychiatrist and family therapy pioneer Murray Bowen took on this issue of closed family systems and grief. He pointed out that within a family, certain deaths can create an emotional "shock wave." In the suicide example in the last paragraph, for instance, the woman who died may have been a strong matriarch of her family, leaving significant gaps functionally and emotionally in her family after her death. Her death may have set in motion a domino effect of other reactions—maybe the children were no longer well cared for; perhaps the family stopped attending church; maybe family meals and gatherings ceased to exist. Such circumstances would be likely to affect the current generation but also future generations. As you get to know a griever and his story, discerning whether the person's death created a shock wave in the family at large—and if so, in which ways that affected the griever—will help you tailor your care accordingly.

"After my unmarried uncle died of a sudden heart attack, it came out that he had sexually abused some of the other nieces—my cousins—when we were children. My mother and her remaining siblings fought and blamed each other about this at first, but then just stopped talking about it. Later on, after my mother died, I learned that my uncle had abused her too. The abuse and the pattern of secrecy has had lifelong repercussions for my family."

11. THE GRIEVER'S PARTICIPATION IN MEANINGFUL CEREMONIES

The funeral ritual and other ceremonies that honor the loss and remember the person who died can have a major influence on a griever's grief journey. In my estimation, this risk factor for complicated grief is often underestimated.

"My family thought it would be easier, faster, and cheaper if we just had a little party when my brother died. In hindsight, I found out that as we tried to be happy and celebrate, we never allowed ourselves to mourn. It has been like I was on hold with my grief for all of these years."

Contrary to popular belief, the funeral is not a rite of closure but a rite of initiation. A full, personalized, inclusive, timely funeral that provides ample opportunities to dose those in attendance with the six needs of mourning, which we'll examine in Part Three, helps put the griever on a healthy path to healing. No funeral, on the other hand, or a cookie-cutter service, does not give mourners a good start. Nor does a service that the griever did not attend. Rushed ceremonies and those that are long delayed are usually insufficient as well. The trend toward party-style memorial services is also detrimental, as these parties typically do not help grievers acknowledge the reality of the death and encounter the pain of the loss.

When the time is right, ask the

Transcendence
Meaning
Expression
Support
Recall
Reality

THE HIERARCHY OF PURPOSES OF FUNERALS

griever to tell you about the funeral experience for the person who died. A bad or nonexistent funeral experience may well be a contributor. We'll be talking more about the power of ritual in Part Three. While the original funeral can't be redone, it is never too late to hold another funeral and/or additional ceremonies. In fact, I find this is one of the most effective tools in the companion's toolkit. I have helped a number of complicated grievers with what I term "corrective emotional ritual experiences."

12. THE GRIEVER'S GRIEF COUNSELING EXPERIENCE TO DATE

Some complicated grievers will come to you with a history of grief counseling. As part of your discovery and history-taking process, it is important, of course, for you to understand what this grief counseling or support consisted of, any progress or regress the griever may have experienced during this time, and which if any grief insights or misconceptions the griever may have incorporated as a result of the counseling.

As we have discussed, our society promulgates a number of harmful misconceptions about grief, including the old saws that grievers simply need to find a way to get over it and move on and that grief is a sign of weakness of faith. In addition, some traditional mental-health caregivers have been so contaminated by their training that they dominate grievers with their "expertise," direct a griever's every move, project a need for closure or a return to homeostasis, and generally run roughshod over a griever's truth and unique risk factors and symptoms.

Between the socio-cultural influences and caregivers' misguided guidance, you will find that some grievers' grief has been, ironically, complicated by grief counseling. In fact, sometimes this risk factor alone is enough to turn what may have been normal grief into complicated grief. It's sad, but it's also true.

As you companion complicated grievers, you may encounter additional influences and risk factors for complicated grief that I have not covered here. Certainly you will meet grievers with numerous idiosyncratic, complicating circumstances. That is how love is, that is how life is, and that is why grief can never effectively be weighed, measured, or placed on a scale of any kind. I also believe it can never be properly supported with lockstep, manualized therapies in which one size fits all. Each instance of grief is unique, and as I have emphasized, all grief is already complicated.

Next, in Part Two, we'll be exploring common care-eliciting symptoms of complicated grief. If the influences and risk factors are the forces that over the course of the griever's life create the exceptionally challenging topography of the wilderness of complicated grief, the symptoms and presentations are the griever's in-the-now responses to that topography. How each griever thinks, feels, and behaves as he moves through the rugged wilderness of his complicated grief are signs for us search-and-rescuers to watch for. We meet the stuck or lost griever where he is, then we bear witness to his story. We listen, watch, empathize, and learn. And only then do we begin to look for opportunities to help him find a way forward.

Questions for reflection and understanding

I invite you to answer the following questions. Writing down your thoughts will help you understand and remember the concepts as well as integrate them with your unique methods of helping grievers.

Which societal contributors have I seen contribute to complicated grief? How so?

Which grief misconceptions have I seen contribute to complicated grief? How so?

Which death circumstances have I seen contribute to complicated grief? How so?

Which relationship characteristics have I seen contribute to complicated grief? How so?

Which secondary losses have I seen contribute to complicated grief? How so?

Which loss history facets have I seen contribute to complicated grief? How so?

In what ways have I seen grievers' access to and use of support contribute to complicated grief? How so?

Which other concurrent stressors in grievers' lives have I seen contribute to complicated grief? How so?

Which facets of grievers' cultural/ethnic backgrounds have I seen contribute to complicated grief? How so?

Which facets of grievers' religious/spiritual/philosophical backgrounds have I seen contribute to complicated grief? How so?

Which family systems influences have I seen contribute to complicated grief? How so?

In what ways have I seen grievers' participation in meaningful ceremonies contribute to complicated grief? How so?

In what ways have I seen grievers' grief counseling experiences to date contribute to complicated grief? How so?

What other risk factors for complicated grief have I seen in my own life experience, my professional training, and my therapy practice? How so?

PART TWO

Identifying Complicated Grief— Symptoms and Categories

In the bereavement caregiver trainings I instruct, students often ask me how to tell if a griever needs professional help. They want to know what normal grief looks like and how to know when it has crossed over into complicated grief. This isn't an easy question. As we've discussed, it's one that has confounded leaders in this field for decades.

In Part One we explored the ways in which grief is influenced by a multitude of factors. Essentially, each instance of grief is unique based on these influences. But given the uniqueness of grief, is it possible to identify when grief tips from normal to complicated? That is the focus of Part Two.

After a significant loss, it's normal for people to experience a wide range of thoughts and feelings. We call these thoughts and feelings grief. They also exhibit a dizzying variety of behaviors. We call these behaviors mourning.

Not only are there many different thoughts, feelings, and behaviors in grief, there is also a continuum of nuance and amplitude for the thoughts, feelings, and behaviors. For instance, many grievers feel angry at some point, but the degree of anger ranges from mild irritation to full-on rage—sometimes within the same individual. And even for an individual griever, feelings routinely come and go, wax and wane.

Similarly, in different mourners the behaviors associated with a feeling may run the gamut from complete inexpression to, again using the example of anger, violent acting-out—and the magnitude of the outward presentation, or mourning, does not always align with the magnitude of the inner feeling. In other words, some people express their feelings proportionately to what they feel inside, and some do not. In fact, many grievers suppress the outward expression of intense inner feelings altogether or temper them significantly.

What's more, intense inner feelings sometimes find outer expression in tangential, unrecognizable, or off-trail ways. This can be challenging for the companion to discern, and often the griever herself is unaware of both the underlying emotion and the connection between the emotion and the behavior. We'll be talking more about this common complicated grief phenomenon later in this section.

As you arrive to companion a particular griever at a particular point in the wilderness of her grief, it's important to keep all of this in mind. I've emphasized that grief is always complicated. It's multidimensional and constantly changing. The fact that it's both inward and outward, proportionate and disproportionate, as well as ever-changing, only makes it more complex. This normal and natural complexity is the backdrop against which we will review the common care-eliciting symptoms and presentations of complicated grief in this section.

Yes, I believe that the thoughts, feelings, and behaviors that grievers share with us and that we are able to sense when we are in their presence are care-eliciting symptoms. While the term "symptom" is indeed associated with the medical-model of health care, I do not think of grief symptoms in this sense. Rather, I believe they are soul-based expressions that I am privileged to bear witness to and honor. Too often, grief symptoms are seen as negative constructs. The so-called "dark emotions" are viewed as pathology that must be eliminated when in fact they are functional responses. I also think of grief symptoms as care-eliciting, which means that whether the griever is aware of it or not, these normal and natural symptoms are signals to others that the griever requires care and compassion from others.

Before we begin the review of the symptoms, I also want to include a reminder that we as companions must be on the watch for the symptoms to express themselves in myriad ways. As they tell you their stories, grievers will sometimes clearly name a feeling: "I still feel so numb, even four years after the death." But as you know, it's more common for grievers to share a feeling without naming it or by describing a behavior that expresses an underlying symptom.

What's more, I am primarily explaining these symptoms as emotions, but they may express themselves not only emotionally but also—or instead—physically, cognitively, socially, and/or spiritually. For example, anxiety is a common grief symptom, but any given griever may not tell you, "I feel anxious." Instead, she may describe feeling physically restless, unable to sit down or accomplish a task. Or she may say she's struggling with reconciling her faith with the death and that her spiritual ruminations have taken over her life. Anxiety by any other mode of expression is still anxiety.

As a trained mental-health caregiver, you are used to employing such discernment, of course, but complicated grief—comprising as it does so many different thoughts, feelings, and behaviors—is a sprawling and complex experience. As I have been emphasizing, it often defies neat labels and categories. Don't be surprised to find that some of the complicated grievers in your care are struggling in multiple ways in varying degrees.

Now let's review the common care-eliciting symptoms and presentations of complicated grief. **14**

Shock, numbness, denial, and disbelief

It's normal for people to feel a sense of shock and numbness when someone they love dies. This is true whether the death was anticipated or unanticipated, though, understandably, the shock is typically more pronounced after an unanticipated death.

As with shock after a physical injury, the shock of grief protects the newly bereaved. It prevents them from having to embrace the full reality of the death all at once. It's a necessary cushion or emotional bubble-wrap, because without it, the psyche would simply be too overwhelmed. Like novocaine, the experience of shock allows the worst pain to come on gradually, over time. Short-term denial functions similarly. It helps grievers survive the early days and weeks.

In complicated grief, these symptoms often persist beyond the early days and weeks and stretch into months and even years. In essence, complicated grievers may be "stuck" in shock and denial. It's common for them to say that they still can't truly believe or accept what happened.

Not only do the shock and denial typically last longer in complicated grief, but they may be more pronounced. One woman whose young adult son died by suicide told me that she likes to think of him living his happy life a few states away. While she is not in literal denial that he is dead, she relies on a sort of fantasy to prolong the protection of her numbness and disbelief. She has acknowledged the reality of the death with her head but not with her heart.

Understandably, in ambiguous loss circumstances it can be especially hard for grievers to fully acknowledge the death. In cases when no body is recovered, or when the body is considered too damaged for viewing, or when grievers, for whatever reason, choose not to view the body, they often run the risk of suffering ongoing feelings of shock and numbness.

I have also seen protracted shock and numbness among grievers who so far have been unable to accept the circumstances of the death. This may occur after suicide, homicide, accidental death, and situations in which the griever somehow contributed to the death.

Disorganization, confusion, searching, and yearning

Grievers often feel distracted and befuddled. As I often say, all change starts with chaos. They describe not being able to focus, concentrate, or think straight. They also yearn and search for the person who died. Searching usually takes the form of expecting the person to walk in the door, looking for the person in the places they would have frequented, and catching glimpses of the person in crowds or passing cars.

In early grief, grievers' minds and hearts are still trying to come to terms with the physical and existential reality of the separation. How can someone who was here suddenly be here no longer? "Where did he go?" grievers often ask, even when they have seen the body in the casket and the casket lowered into the ground. The concept of "goneness" seems unfathomable, and it often takes a great deal of time and attention to get used to.

Some risk factors can make this dimension of normal grief longer or more severe, including (but not limited to) challenging death circumstances and extreme dependence in the relationship. As you can imagine, ambiguous, violent, or surreal loss circumstances often result in chaotic and disorganized thinking. When it seems like the fundamental laws of nature have been violated, our minds are naturally discombobulated and distracted. And the stronger the attachment and the more day-in-and-day-out time the griever spent with the person who died before the death, the more intense and frequent the griever's searching and yearning is likely to be.

A continued relationship after death

Throughout most of the 20th century, multiple grief luminaries declared that one important task grievers had to undertake and complete was to "let go" of the person who died. Healthy grievers, they said, achieved closure. The thinkers, mostly prominent psychiatrists we have already mentioned in this book, believed that continued love after death was a pathology, part of the pathological or morbid grief diagnosis.

This never made sense to me, and I began speaking and writing about the misconception of "closure" and "letting go" early in my career. From my own personal experience as well as the first grievers I companioned, I knew that grievers did not "get over" grief but rather were permanently changed by it and lived with it forever.

In 1996, researchers Dr. Dennis Klass, Dr. Phyllis Silverman, and Dr. Steven Nickman proposed the theory of continuing bonds, which says that we don't "let go" of the person who died after all but rather continue to love the person who died while integrating the fact of their death and the nature of the changed relationship. Their theory is now widely accepted. My own writings and teaching have always reflected this reality. As Morrie Schwartz of the bestselling Mitch Albom memoir *Tuesdays with Morrie* famously said, "Death ends a life, not a relationship."

Of course. Grievers continue to love the people who died. Every griever finds a way of thinking about and expressing this. This is an appropriate way of honoring those who have gone before us. In fact, honoring means valuing, cherishing, and holding dear. Some routinely talk aloud to the person who died. Some believe the dead person is quite literally watching over them. Some are sure that the person is waiting for them in heaven and that they will be reunited one day. Among those who don't believe in an afterlife, I have noticed it's still common to think of the person who died as continuing on in some form.

Among both normal and complicated grievers, you will see a range and variety of continuing relationships with those who have died. There are only two kinds that concern me. One is when the griever feels that without the physical presence of the person who died, he cannot find his way to new meaning in life or experience joy again. The other is when the griever acts as if the ongoing relationship with the person who died precludes him from strengthening other and forming new relationships with living humans. These are complicated grief presentations that require your understanding and mourning support.

Grief, time, and griefbursts

As we discuss complicated grief symptoms in this section, I want you to tuck a few important general concepts into the back of your mind.

In general, a griever's normal grief symptoms soften over time as a result of active mourning and the support of others. In other words, normal grief attenuates. It never goes away completely, but it fades into the background, becoming an inextricable part of the fabric of the griever's life.

Note that time alone does not heal grief. That is a misconception. Actually, as I often teach, grief waits on welcome, not on time.

Complicated grief also softens, but for that to happen, the griever usually needs more help and support in his grief journey. That's where you come in. The time and energy required of the griever are also more substantial. Healing complicated grief is slower and takes longer.

In both normal and complicated grief, some of the symptoms we are reviewing in Part Two will not disappear completely (which symptoms depends on the unique griever), and occasionally they will resurge dramatically. I call this phenomenon "griefbursts."

Griefbursts are normal flares of grief that intermittently arise long after the death. Some authors refer to these as grief attacks, but I prefer the term griefbursts, because the term "attack" pathologizes, similar to the term "panic attack." Griefbursts may seem dramatic, both to the griever and to others—including you, the grief companion—but they are normal. At a reminder of the loss, such as a place or a smell, or even out of the blue, a griever may find herself sobbing, floored by a memory, or overcome with profound sadness.

Of course, talking about the loss will also bring on griefbursts, so, as you know, they are a common experience in the grief companion's office.

I would caution, however, that in my professional experience, griefbursts are not primarily indicative of complicated grief. They happen just as often in normal grief, especially in the grief-encounter setting that is the therapist's office. Yes, they are pronounced, heightened feelings, and yes, we have said that feature prominence may indicate complicated grief, but I urge you to use discernment regarding griefbursts.

A wound hurts when it is prodded, whether it is a small wound or a larger wound. Just because a griever responds with labile emotionality in your presence or describes griefbursts that have overtaken her recently doesn't necessarily mean the grief is complicated or that you need to be concerned about what are typically termed and may legitimately be "comorbid mental-health pathologies." Grief is normal. Complicated grief is normal. And griefbursts are normal.

One final caveat: Living in a state of griefburst is not normal. Grievers who report that they experience more-or-less constant griefbursts are often stuck in encamped grief (see pg. 122). Healthy grief and mourning involves encountering then evading, evading then encountering. With the possible exception of the early hours and days immediately following the death, it is an intermittent process.

Anxiety, panic, and fear

Death naturally arouses a plethora of anxieties and fears in all of us. As C.S. Lewis astutely observed, "I did not know that grief felt so much like fear." Questions tug at our minds and hearts. What happens after death? Will I be OK? When and how will I die? What about others I love? What if they die soon too? How will I go on without the person who died?

These are the Big Questions of life and death, for which there are no easy answers. But in a time of death, the little uncertainties vex us too. Who will clean out the person's room or house? What should be done with her belongings? How will the paperwork get completed? Is there enough money to pay the bills?

Grievers who struggled with anxiety, panic, and fear before the death are, of course, predisposed to be more challenged by this dimension after the death. Any medical treatment they may have received in the past for anxiety or panic attacks should be reassessed and possibly continued or modified.

In addition, violent or otherwise frightening death circumstances may engender a traumatic grief response that in essence splits the grief into two components: post-traumatic stress and grief. The traumatic component serves to complicate the grief and may benefit from trauma processing—a technique that is outside the purview of this text but may be an essential skill in your toolkit or a point of differentiation for referral.

Traumatic grief and fear 18

If the event that caused a griever's loss (in PTSD parlance, this is called the "stressor") is violent and/or sudden and unexpected, when we are speaking of the loss in the vernacular we often conjure the term "traumatic." Being injured in a car crash (sudden and violent) is traumatic. The death of a loved one to suicide or homicide (violent and sometimes but not always sudden) is traumatic. In general, the more violent the loss experience, the more traumatic we consider it. (But remember, the perception of what is and is not a traumatic death is subjective.)

Note that violent traumatic events first and foremost threaten the bottom two layers of Maslow's famous pyramid. They compromise the bodies and the safety of ourselves or of those we care about. They activate the fight, flight, or freeze fear response that is central to what has been termed post-traumatic stress disorder, or PTSD.

MASLOW'S
HIERARCHY OF NEEDS

Self-actualization

Esteem

Social

Safety

Physiological

In the past, the *Diagnostic and Statistical Manual* classified PTSD among anxiety disorders. Today, the *DSM-5* has moved PTSD to a new category called "trauma- and stressor-related disorders." In the case of PTSD, the primary symptoms involve the re-experiencing or repeated intrusion of the event. The remaining symptoms involve avoidance, negative cognition and mood, and hyper-arousal.

Essentially, the traumatic nature of the loss creates a unique, two-part grief experience: one focused on the event itself, and one focused on the losses the event created. This is a form of complicated grief!

In short, I would say that traumatic grief and what is called PTSD are part of the same continuum, with PTSD inhabiting the extreme far end of the bell curve. Further, I would suggest that the label "post-traumatic stress disorder" implies an illness where actually there is what could be considered a normal (albeit stuck) response to an abnormally severe psychic injury.

Once again, the word "disorder" is being used to pathologize a form of grief.

I believe that the term "traumatic grief" actually captures better than the term "PTSD" the totality of people's experience following traumatic loss. "PTSD" is all about the event of the loss, whereas "traumatic grief" acknowledges both the traumatic event and the entirety of the grief journey that ensues. Grievers experiencing traumatic grief need special care, which I will address in Part Three.

Explosive emotions

Anger, hate, blame, terror, resentment, rage, and jealousy are explosive emotions that can naturally take hold of many grievers. It helps to understand that in grief, these feelings are fundamentally a form of protest. The griever is struggling to accept the reality of the death (and perhaps the circumstances of the death) as well as the consequences of the death. She does not want them to be true. She wants the death not to have happened. Her explosive emotions essentially express, "No! This is NOT OK with me!"

As you know, underlying explosive emotions are usually deeper, more challenging feelings of pain, helplessness, frustration, and fear. The more active explosive emotions feel relatively good in comparison, so grievers will often unconsciously turn first to them instead.

While explosive emotions in grief are normal and common, pronounced, prolonged, and/or acted-upon explosive emotions should be considered facets of complicated grief. For example, one griever I companioned presented with bitter anger over the death of his only child—anger that had not softened in the years since she died. He carried an intense perceived injustice over the fact that his daughter had preceded him in death. It just wasn't fair, he believed. Though he felt just and paternal in his wrath, his anger was causing problems in his life. He had been repeatedly fired from jobs over anger management issues. His relationship with his wife was in tatters. It turned out that he needed my help encountering the second need of mourning (see pg. 162)—embracing the pain of the loss—as well as several others. His anger was shielding him from all of the needs of mourning—and thus from reconciliation and healing. During our time together, he began to embrace the pain underlying his anger, and his work and personal life began to improve. His protest emotions softened, and he returned to a healthy mourning path.

When "support" is irritating

Grievers are often angered by the bromides others offer them in response to their loss. "Words of wisdom," usually spoken by well-intentioned people who want to voice their support, often have the opposite effect. Instead of feeling supported, grievers feel denigrated and misunderstood.

Here are just a few of the common true-but-not-helpful platitudes grievers often hear:

- At least you had him for 50 years.
- He lived a good, long life.
- You have other children. (Or: You can have other children.)
- God wouldn't give you anything more than you can bear.
- One door closes, another one opens.

Bromides and clichés in the guise of grief support may complicate grief if they're the primary messages that a griever is hearing. This is an example of dissonance between the truth of what the griever is feeling inside and the mirror in which the outside world is reflecting back her grief. When the dissonance becomes too overbearing or pervasive, the griever may understandably get mired in anger and confusion. Interestingly, as they struggle with this dissonance and react with anger, they're often perceived by others as "not handling their grief well." This is a form of secondary victimization in grief, and unfortunately I have seen it occur many times.

Explosive emotions that find expression in destructive ways are also red flags for complicated grief. Self-harm, extreme risk-taking, harm to others, and harm to property all cross the line. Often, the circumstances of the loss combined with the personality and life history of the griever make the destructiveness somewhat understandable, but when it impinges on safety or violates social norms (not to mention the law), it is incumbent on the grief companion to help the griever befriend her explosive emotions, encounter what may be beneath them, and find means of expression that are constructive and safe.

Another source of explosive emotions in grievers can be resentment over a sense of having been unfairly affected by loss. Understandably, people who experience any number of the complicated grief risk factors we discussed in Part One, such as before-time death, violent or self-inflicted death, or loss overload, may feel a sense of injustice not only on their own behalf, but also on behalf of others affected by the loss and even the person who died. What's more, some grievers resent still being alive when someone else—who may have been younger, healthier, "needed," or "better"—has died. While sometimes this feeling presents as guilt, at other times it takes the form of anger and even rage at the perceived injustice.

Clean pain versus dirty pain ⑲

I like to use the phrase "clean pain" to describe the normal pain that follows difficult life experiences. "Dirty pain" is the damaging, multiplied pain people create when they catastrophize, judge themselves, or allow themselves to be judged by others. Dirty pain is the story they tell themselves about the clean pain.

I would say that normal grief is clean pain. But when a particular aspect of the grief becomes exaggerated and stuck, dirty pain is often, at least in part, the culprit. For example, grievers who tell themselves a potentially inaccurate story about the cause of the death or a rationale for the death may be grappling with dirty pain that is complicating their grief.

If the person died by suicide, let's say, and the griever blames others for having made the person upset enough to take his own life, this ongoing blame and anger can become a source of complicated grief. And yet, we know that such blame is often an invented narrative; the story the griever is telling himself may or may not have actually had anything to do with the death, or it may have played a much smaller role than he realizes.

I once counseled a woman who had divorced her husband because the relationship was not healthy. After the divorce, he took his own life. Perhaps understandably, the woman struggled with ongoing feelings of guilt, which were reinforced by others in her life who vocally blamed her for her ex-husband's death. I helped her understand that most of her guilt was dirty pain.

Grief companions who detect dirty pain have the opportunity to, slowly and gently, help these grievers tell themselves a new story. Don't get me wrong—the dirty-pain story is also valid, simply because it exists. The griever's reality is always her reality. But in encountering and bearing witness to the dirty-pain story, the companion can often help grievers understand that there are other ways—just as valid but also more constructive—to interpret and incorporate what happened.

My professional experience has shown me that in the wilderness of grief, dirty pain can make a mountain out of a molehill. As companion, you can help grievers see these mirage mountains for what they are and ultimately traverse them with more confidence and ease.

Guilt, regret, and self-blame

Guilt, regret, and self-blame are natural feelings after the death of someone loved. Normal grief often includes "if-onlys": "If only I had told him…" "If only I had brought her to a different doctor…" "If only I hadn't…" Often such feelings are not logical, but they torment grievers nonetheless. Why? Because grief is anchored in love, not logic.

In normal grief, guilt and regret almost always stem from feelings of love, because love and relationships typically involve some degree of mutual responsibility and caretaking. In other words, when I love someone and she loves me, we look out for each other. And certain relationships, such as parent-to-child, are built on caretaking. Thus, when someone I care for dies, I may feel partly or vaguely responsible, to some degree, for what happened, even though I am not literally responsible for the death.

WHEN GRIEF IS COMPLICATED

What's more, none of us is perfect, and so we all have regrets about mistakes we made in our relationships, things we did or didn't do, etc. It's normal to regret such mistakes or unreconciled issues when absolution or correction is rendered impossible by death.

Subtypes of guilt often seen in grievers are:

- *survivor guilt*—in which the griever feels guilty for still being alive when the person who died is not.

- *relief-guilt*—in which, commonly after a terminal illness, the griever feels relief that a long period of suffering is over yet also guilty about the sense of relief.

- *joy-guilt*—in which the griever feels guilty whenever he experiences anything pleasurable in the midst of his grief. (Some complicated grievers consciously decide to never be happy again. See encamped grief, page 122.)

- *magical-thinking guilt*—in which the griever feels guilty for having wished at some point that the person would suffer/go away/die or the relationship would be over.

- *longstanding, personality-related guilt*—in which the griever, often as a result of family-of-origin dynamics, feels responsible whenever something bad happens.

All such thoughts and feelings are common and normal in grief, but they are also typically transitory and attenuating. They come and go, they tend to be subordinate to other feelings, and they also soften with time and expression.

In complicated grief, guilt and regret may dominate, and they may not soften over time. In short, they may act as a quicksand in which a griever gets stuck. In my companioning experience, the more complicated grief risk factors a griever possesses, the more likely he is to harbor profound guilt and regret that are responsible, at least in part, for causing his normal grief to balloon into complicated grief.

Deaths separating hyper-dependent people can heighten feelings of guilt, and sometimes, past mistakes and unreconciled issues are so extreme that the normal regrets that follow death are also extreme. For example, if the abused person in a relationship dies, the abuser may struggle with secret guilt. Or, if a narcissistic parent dies, her child may become mired in regrets—that he didn't have a more loving mother, that he continued to be manipulated by her and never set boundaries, that his own children didn't have the grandmother he wanted them to have, etc.

Guilt is also a common grief feature following circumstances in which the family was forced to decide whether or not to remove life support or use extraordinary means to keep a loved one alive. Various family members may have felt differently about the outcome. What's more, these situations are often crises, and determinations have to be made quickly, while family members are in shock and may even lack full understanding. In hindsight, what seemed like a reasonable decision at the time may later feel much grayer and more regrettable.

In addition, sometimes complicated grievers harbor guilt for having *actually* contributed to the death in some way. I know of a tragic situation in which one brother accidentally killed another brother, for example. His grief, and his family's grief, cannot help but be complicated by the tragedy of this circumstance.

I once companioned a grieving man whose wife was killed in a car accident. He and his wife had been driving a long distance, and in an effort to save money, he had decided to continue driving through the night rather than stop and pay for a motel. He fell asleep at the wheel. He naturally wrestled with his guilt over her death, but he also struggled with the advice of a number of people around him who told him, "You didn't mean to do it. It was an accident." In our time together, I created a holding environment to help him acknowledge that he had made a bad decision, own his appropriate guilt, and eventually forgive himself.

Sadness and depression

Sadness and depression are natural, authentic emotions after a loss. It's normal for grievers to feel profound pain and a muting of desire and pleasure. Yet these are among the most challenging emotions for grievers to befriend, especially in a culture that vilifies pain and encourages "getting over it" as quickly as possible. "She wouldn't want you to be sad!" is the oft-repeated refrain.

In grief, sadness and depression play an essential role. They force us to regroup—physically, cognitively, emotionally, socially, and spiritually. When we are sad, we instinctively turn inward. We withdraw. We slow down. It's as if our soul presses the pause button and says, "Whoa, whoa, whoaaa. Time out. I need to acknowledge what's happened here."

The necessary sadness of grief can also be referred to as "sitting in your wound." When you sit in the wound of your grief, you surrender to it. You acquiesce to the instinct to slow down and turn inward. You allow yourself to appropriately wallow in the pain. You shut out the world for a time so that, eventually, you have created space and energy to let the world back in.

Even in normal grief, it often takes weeks or months before grievers arrive at the full depth of their sorrow. I have observed that the pain almost always gets worse before it gets better. This fits with the organic, recursive nature of grief. And so, profound sadness and depression may be considered normal and necessary. But as with the other dimensions we've been reviewing in this section, sadness and depression may be sufficiently debilitating or prolonged in some grievers to be considered markers of complicated grief. Clinical depression, of course, is also a serious consideration, which we will now introduce.

Complicated grief or clinical depression? [20]

According to the Centers for Disease Control, at any given time one in ten American adults is clinically depressed, and one in 25 meets the criteria for major depression. Throughout their lifetimes, one-fourth of all Americans will experience at least one episode of depression.

Are these numbers falsely inflated by the trend toward the medicalization of normal existential troubles? Probably. But while I worry that we are diagnosing clinical depression too liberally because we as a culture misunderstand the role of pain and suffering, I am not a depression denier. I do believe that clinical depression is a real physical disorder that may require medical treatment.

As you know, a number of influences may play a role in the development of clinical depression, including genetics, stress (such as a significant loss), and changes in body and brain function. What's more, many people with clinical depression have low levels of certain brain chemicals and slower cellular activity in parts of the brain that control mood, appetite, sleep, and other functions.

To review, in the *DSM-5*, Major Depressive Disorder can be diagnosed when five (or more) of the following symptoms a) represent a change from previous functioning *and* b) have been present for at least two weeks:

1. Depressed mood most of the day, nearly every day

2. Little pleasure in all or most activities

3. Significant weight loss or gain

4. Insomnia or hypersomnia

5. Physical agitation or lethargy

6. Fatigue or loss of energy

7. Feelings of worthlessness or excessive guilt

8. Inability to think, concentrate, or decide

9. Recurring thoughts of death or suicide

Symptom numbers 1 and/or 2 must be present for the depression to be considered MDD, and the patient must also be in "clinically significant distress" or impaired functionally in social, occupational, or other areas.

The trouble for us grief companions is that depression and grief look a lot alike. Most normal grief symptoms overlap with clinical depression symptoms, let alone complicated grief symptoms, which are even more likely to mimic clinical depression. In fact, in the *DSM-5* list above, all nine symptoms may also be present in complicated grief.

When it comes to grief, complicated or not, I (and many other professional caregivers, I will note) take issue with the two-week timeframe in the *DSM-5*. Previous *DSMs* excluded newly bereaved people from a major depression diagnosis, but the *DSM-5* removed this exclusion. Now, even in normal grief, many grievers would meet the criteria for MDD given this timeframe.

Proponents argue that removing the bereavement exclusion allows clinicians to quickly treat mourners who are clinically depressed and may be suicidal. It's true—sometimes grievers react so dramatically to the death of a loved one that they may be in immediate danger to themselves. In these cases, short-term hospitalization or other interventions may indeed be required, and taking all professional precautions to help prevent a griever's suicide is a necessary standard of care. I urge you to stay current with the proper resources and protocols in your community for the care of suicidal people.

Still, it is common for grievers, normal or complicated, to entertain passive thoughts of suicide. This usually takes the form of the griever wishing he wouldn't wake up in the morning, wishing he had died instead, or wishing he could fast-forward through the pain and on to his own death. I believe that for these grievers, such thoughts are often a necessary part of their journey. They must befriend the idea of their own death before they are able to choose to live again. But actual suicide is another matter entirely. What we must be on the lookout for in the grievers we companion are suicidal thoughts that take on planning and action.

Warning signs of suicide ㉓

For grief companions who are committed to the principles of non-medicalized, soul-based care for grievers, the prospect of suicide among those in our care remains a sobering possibility. As all mental-health clinicians do, we must remain vigilant for the warning signs and refer grievers for additional or different care when their needs surpass or fall outside our expertise.

Here are the warning signs of suicide as I describe them to grievers and their families. I have found that lay language can sometimes reawaken professional caregivers to the normalcy and humanity of these symptoms.

_____ A sudden switch from being very sad to being very calm or appearing to be happy

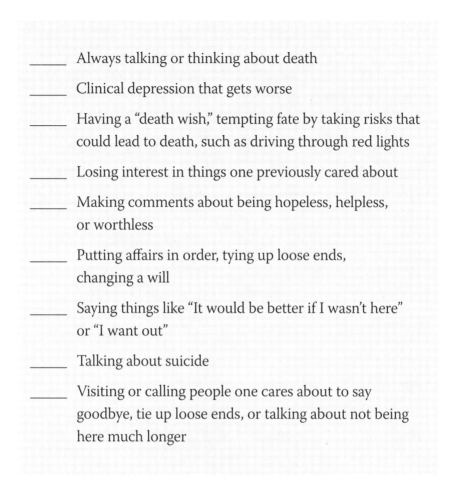

_____ Always talking or thinking about death

_____ Clinical depression that gets worse

_____ Having a "death wish," tempting fate by taking risks that could lead to death, such as driving through red lights

_____ Losing interest in things one previously cared about

_____ Making comments about being hopeless, helpless, or worthless

_____ Putting affairs in order, tying up loose ends, changing a will

_____ Saying things like "It would be better if I wasn't here" or "I want out"

_____ Talking about suicide

_____ Visiting or calling people one cares about to say goodbye, tie up loose ends, or talking about not being here much longer

Suicidal ideation aside, though, trying to tease apart what is clinical depression and what is complicated grief can feel like splitting hairs. One area to pay particular attention to is feelings of self-worth. While people who are grieving a death often feel guilty over some aspect of the relationship or the circumstances of the death, as we have already discussed, they do not typically feel worthless. In other words, people with complicated grief may feel guilty and even hopeless for a time, while people with clinical depression often feel a more generalized low sense of self-worth and hopelessness.

In addition, grievers who have suffered from clinical depression in the past, before coming to grief or apart from loss, should be closely monitored for clinical depression after a loss and potentially treated proactively. Be sure to encourage anyone who is currently taking antidepressants for properly diagnosed depression to stay on them. Sometimes the natural confusion and lethargy of grief interfere with medication compliance.

The bottom line is that **the boundaries that separate normal grief, complicated grief, traumatic grief, and clinical depression are blurry and somewhat arbitrary**. In determining how best to help struggling grievers, grief companions must always use their most careful judgment, both clinical and nonclinical.

If the griever meets the *DSM* criteria for clinical depression, including functional impairment, medical treatment should be considered *in addition to* intensive companioning. Even if the depression can be attributed wholly to the loss, the griever may need relief from her depressive symptoms in order to more fully engage with the needs of mourning and reclaim hope.

Normal grief or complicated grief?

As we have said, grief is a continuum of normal thoughts, feelings, and behaviors. When a certain feature becomes pronounced or stuck, we may consider the grief complicated. There are a lot of gray areas, though, and for the most part, because all grief is complicated, I am reluctant to say, "This is complicated grief" and "This is normal grief."

Still, I have created this at-a-glance chart for you to refer to as you try to discern whether or not—and if so, how—a particular griever's journey is extra complicated.

The darker gray rows in this chart are important and unique. Unlike the risk factors in the other rows, the items in dark gray are those I consider more definitional of complicated grief. In other words, someone who exhibits a feature highlighted in dark gray in the definitional features column is likely experiencing complicated grief.

The remaining risk factors are not absolutes. I've placed a history of mental illness in the complicated grief column, for example, but that doesn't mean that someone with a history of depression will necessarily end up with complicated grief. It simply means that this person may be at higher risk for complicated grief. What's more, the risk factors often compound one another. The more risk factors a griever has, the more likely she is to experience complicated grief after a significant loss.

NORMAL GRIEF Definitional features	COMPLICATED GRIEF Definitional features
After the initial period of shock and the funeral and the first several months or so, the griever is able to function in his daily life for the most part, even while grieving.	After the initial period of shock and the funeral and the first several months or so, the griever is still unable to function in his daily life as a result of his grief.
Softens and eases over time.	Seems stuck at a level of intensity and/or dimensions exhibited.

(continued)	(continued)
In early days, shock and numbness are prevalent.	Prolonged shock and numbness prevail over an extended period of time. Grief and/or mourning may seem absent.
Feelings shift and change, with different thoughts and emotions becoming more prominent at different times.	One or two grief dimensions seem to dominate (e.g., anger), and this does not change over time, nor do the prominent dimensions soften.
The griever's expressed thoughts, feelings, and behaviors seem to align with what you might expect given the particular loss.	The greiver's expressed thoughts, feelings, and behaviors seem inappropriate or out-of-proportion given the particular loss (e.g., risk-taking behaviors or acting out revenge fantasies) or even tangential to the loss (e.g., the greiver who immediately invests her love and energy in a new relationship instead of mourning the loss of the previous relationship).

WHEN GRIEF IS COMPLICATED

The griever is not turning to addictive behaviors as a method of self-treating the pain.	The griever is turning to addictive behaviors as a method of self-treating the pain.
Loss situation—lower-risk	**Loss situation—higher-risk**
Often follows an expected and/or natural-order loss.	Often follows a loss that is especially traumatic for one or more reasons, or multiple losses within a relatively short period of time.
The griever's relationship with the person who died was healthy and loving.	The griever's relationship with the person who died was unusually close (possibly hyper-dependent), or characterized by abuse or conflict, or ambivalence.
The griever has no significant history of mental illness.	The griever has a history of mental illness.
The griever is able to access and express emotionality.	The griever has trouble accessing and expressing emotionality.
The griever's cultural, ethnic, and religious traditions support grief and mourning.	The griever's cultural, ethnic, and religious traditions don't support grief and mourning.

(continued)	(continued)
The griever has good support systems.	The griever has inadequate support systems.
The griever spent time with the body (if culturally appropriate) and experienced a full, loving, personalized funeral for the person who died.	The griever did not see or spend time with the body (if culturally appropriate) and/ or did not experience a full, loving, personalized funeral for the person who died.

Carried grief 24

In Part One we explored carried grief as one of the risk factors for complicated grief. As a reminder, carried grief is accumulated grief from life losses that have never been adequately acknowledged and mourned. In this subsection we'll review a set of symptoms that I have often seen associated with carried grief in the mourners I have companioned. Just one, two, or sometimes several symptoms may be present. You will notice some overlap among these symptoms and those we have already covered in Part Two, but here they will be described as features independent of the recent loss—in other words, symptoms that were likely present before the recent loss occurred.

Please note that I have gleaned the list of symptoms we are about to review from my professional experience of 40 years, not hard research. Of course, such symptoms may also be caused by other issues. Anxiety, for example, may also result from thyroid imbalances or preexisting personality or mental-health challenges.

Carried grief symptoms

Difficulties with trust and intimacy

Depression and negative outlook

Anxiety and panic attacks

Psychic numbing and disconnection

Irritability and agitation

Substance abuse, addictions, eating disorders

Physical problems, real or imagined

DIFFICULTIES WITH TRUST AND INTIMACY

Many grief-carriers have taught me that they feel they are
unlovable. Often, this becomes a self-fulfilling prophecy. They are
sometimes aware of the need for love but at the same time feel
unworthy of it. Feelings of being unloved can then translate into
"I am unlovable." The tragic result is often isolation and loneliness.
Some of these people do get married or attempt to have close
relationships but still keep their distance in an effort to stay safe.

Grief-carriers often feel, consciously or subconsciously, that others
will leave them. Those who have been abandoned both by death
and in their need to mourn by the significant people in their lives
naturally feel that others will also abandon them. When they tried
to trust in the past, people betrayed that trust, and they came to
believe no one was trustworthy. They don't open their heart easily,
and when they do, they fear others will misuse them and ultimately
leave. So, it became safer over time to stay distant and closed off.

SADNESS AND DEPRESSION

Grief-carriers often experience an ongoing loss of their divine spark—that which gives purpose and meaning to our living. When the spirit is muted, there is an unending hampering of the capacity to live life with meaning and purpose. The result is often depression and a negative, cynical view of life.

Depression sometimes reveals itself as a generally negative outlook on life. While grief-carriers may certainly experience major depression, I have noticed that they commonly suffer from dysthymia, or chronic, low-grade depression. They lose their full range of emotional functioning, defending against ever being really happy or really sad. Sometimes they rationalize this mood state as "this is just what life is like."

Similarly, feelings of meaninglessness often pervade the lives of grief-carriers. People who grieve but don't mourn often feel isolated emotionally and lack a sense of meaning and purpose. They experience a sense of soullessness or a loss of vitality and enthusiasm for life and living. It's common for them to feel empty and alone.

ANXIETY AND PANIC ATTACKS

Some grief-carriers struggle with a persistent and generalized anxiety. Anxiety is often reflected in motor tension (fatigue, muscle aches, easy startle response); autonomic hyperactivity (dry mouth, gastrointestinal distress, heart racing); apprehensive expectations (fears of injury or death); and hyper-vigilance and scanning (hyper-alertness, irritability, and problems with sleep disturbance). Again, just as with depression, there can be multiple causes of anxiety; however, I am certain that carried pain is a contributor for many people.

Anxiety sometimes shows up in the form of panic attacks. Panic is a sudden, overpowering fright. On occasion, these attacks may last for hours, though attacks are typically only a period of minutes, during which the person literally experiences terror. As you know, panic attacks are often recurrent and episodic, though for some people they become chronic.

The human spirit yearns for connection to others and unconditional love. I have seen numerous people in grief counseling whose panic attacks were the doorway to get them to give attention to carried grief and learn to authentically mourn.

PSYCHIC NUMBING AND DISCONNECTION

While shock and numbness are normal early responses in the face of loss and may be extended in complicated grief, grief-carriers often get so detached that they literally feel disconnected from the world around them for years and decades. These grievers may describe noticing that they can see and hear others around them, but they can't feel them.

The result is that the world and the people in it seem unreal. They may live feeling they are in a daze, going through the motions yet not feeling present to others or even to themselves. Some people describe this as a dream-like state with feelings of unreality. They are existing but not really alive to what is going on around them, even in circumstances that one would normally describe as joyful.

IRRITABILITY AND AGITATION

Some grief-carriers express their pain indirectly through irritability and agitation. These symptoms may show up at work, at home, or anywhere they can find expression. It is as if they are in a pressure cooker, and they are trying to release the pressure. In its extreme form, this symptom may show up as uncontrolled anger or rage.

For grief carriers, these emotions of protest are often an

unconscious attempt to fight off the underlying, more primary emotions of pain, helplessness, hurt, isolation, and aloneness. People around them who sense or experience their irritability and agitation often avoid them, resulting in more carried pain and less authentic mourning.

SUBSTANCE ABUSE, ADDICTIONS, EATING DISORDERS ㉑
Many grief-carriers will self-treat their pain through substance abuse, addictive behaviors, and eating disorders. Modern society provides an increasing number of substances that might be abused. People are usually abusive of or addicted to a specific substance, such as alcohol, cocaine, or food. However, grief-carriers can also be addicted to compulsive activities, such as destructive relationships, sex, smoking, gambling, work, exercise, achievement, over-caretaking of others, religiosity, and materialism. These substances and activities are ways the griever tries to move away from or deny the pain of life losses.

Addictions serve to numb the grief-carrier's feelings, sapping their spirit or "life force," and locking them into living a life that feels muted and lacking in purpose and positive direction. Self-treating carried pain through addictions prevents them from deeper satisfactions and any kind of spiritual fulfillment. And unfortunately, many addictions result in a slow but steady process of self-destruction.

PHYSICAL PROBLEMS, REAL OR IMAGINED
If people don't mourn one way, it comes out another. Many grief-carriers store the pain in their bodies. Stress hormones such as cortisol wreak havoc, especially over the long-term. The result is that the immune system can break down, inflammation may be triggered, and illness and real physical pain often surface.

Alternately, when people shut down, deny, or inhibit mourning, they sometimes assume a "sick role" in an effort to legitimize not feeling well to those around them. They somaticize their feelings of grief, subconsciously turning their emotional and spiritual hurts into physical ones. This often results in frequent visits to the physician's office. Sometimes the physical symptoms are very real; other times they are imagined. These imagined symptoms are like a silent voice crying out for the need to give expression to the carried pain. Typically, there are no organic findings to support a physical diagnosis.

We should note that somaticizing is different than the person who experiences real physical illness after a loss. Studies have documented significant increases in illness following the experience of a variety of losses in life, particularly death loss. However, somaticizing grief as the chief mechanism of mourning is a means of avoiding grief. These grief carriers may truly feel sick, but medically speaking there is not anything really wrong with them. Quite simply, life cannot re-inhabit the body until the losses are mourned. The result is that grief carriers often feel sick, if not dead, while they are alive. The good news is that carried griefs stored in the body can be integrated into life as long as their true causes do not continue to be denied. As carried grievers begin to embrace their emotional and spiritual pain, the bodily pain typically eases.

Complicated grief symptoms summary

Just like normal grief, complicated grief may present with a wide variety of symptoms. Following are the symptoms we've reviewed in Part Two so far:

Shock, numbness, denial, and disbelief

Disorganization, confusion, searching, yearning

Anxiety, panic, fear

Explosive emotions

Guilt and regret

Sadness and depression

    Suicidal ideation

Carried grief

    Difficulties with trust and intimacy

    Depression and negative outlook

    Anxiety and panic attacks

    Psychic numbing and disconnection

    Irritability and agitation

    Substance abuse, addictions, eating disorders

    Physical problems, real or imagined

In my view, there is no valid formula or "point system" for determining whether someone is experiencing complicated grief. Every feature we have discussed may also be a common symptom of "normal" grief. Again, it is a matter of degree, feature prominence, functional impact, and, sometimes, duration, and ultimately it is your judgment call.

Most of all, I urge you to ask yourself: Might this griever benefit from compassionate companioning? A "yes" to this question is the only answer you truly need.

Now that we've reviewed individual symptoms of complicated grief, it's time to turn our attention to subtypes of complicated grief that have been defined by various researchers and clinicians over the decades.

Complicated grief categories ㉗

In the Introduction we briefly reviewed the history of the disciplinary understanding of complicated grief. Throughout the decades, from Freud to the current day, there has also been a concurrent stream of thinking about what are generally called subtypes or categories—and sometimes "syndromes," a term the *DSM* prefers and that I do not like because it further pathologizes—of complicated grief.

In 1937, Dr. Helene Deutsch wrote of "**absent grief**," which in her definition is essentially the same as what I have termed "carried grief"—grief that has never been acknowledged or expressed.

Shortly after, in 1944, Dr. Erich Lindemann described what he called **distorted grief**, with nine presentations: overactivity without a sense of loss; symptoms belonging to the last illness of the deceased; psychosomatic illness; a conspicuous alteration of relationships to friends and relatives; furious hostility against specific people; a wooden and formal demeanor; a lasting loss of patterns of social interaction; actions detrimental to the individual's own social and economic existence; and agitated depression. While I agree that grievers presenting with these symptoms need special care, the rigidity of his categorizations has not held up over time.

In 1963, the British psychiatrist and grief specialist Dr. Colin Murray Parkes identified what he termed **three types of pathological grief—chronic, inhibited, and delayed**. In later years, Parkes also included **unexpected grief syndrome** and **ambivalent grief** as subtypes.

Fast forward to 1993, when in her textbook *Treatment of Complicated Mourning* Dr. Therese Rando enumerated seven complicated grief "syndromes," each with their own descriptions, determinants, associated factors, and treatment issues: **absent, delayed, inhibited, distorted, conflicted, unanticipated, and chronic**. More recently, there seems to be less clinical interest in such categorizing as researchers attempt to nail down definitive criteria for the umbrella syndrome, complicated grief itself—a folly, in my opinion.

Still, over the years, in my clinical practice and through my experiences as a grief educator, I have broken down complicated grief into some of these categories myself, as a helpful shorthand for discussing typical complicated grief responses. But I have recently given them different names that are more in keeping with my strong belief that complicated grief is not a pathology but rather a normal human response to an especially complex loss experience. I present the new terms in this book for the first time, and I hope that they will help you recognize and understand these common presentations.

Unembarked grief

Unembarked grief is grief that has never been allowed to depart from the trailhead and enter the normal and necessary wilderness of grief. Similar to what others have termed "absent," "delayed," or "inhibited" grief, unembarked grief is simply uninitiated or unlaunched grief. Carried grief, which we have already discussed, is a subcategory of unembarked grief.

In the early days after a significant loss, grievers who continue to act as if everything is normal or that nothing has happened are typically experiencing normal shock and numbness. But when these symptoms persist for months and even years, unembarked grief is the likely culprit.

As I've said, short-term denial in the face of the death of a loved one is a lifesaving protective mechanism. Limited denial is our friend. It helps us survive what would otherwise be unsurvivable. But long-term denial essentially deadens grievers. It heightens the risk that they will become the walking dead. Unfortunately, our culture often encourages long-term denial and unembarked grief with messages such as "You're doing really well" and "You're so strong." Our short social norms for mourning (three days!) also contribute to this phenomenon.

Grievers who have never learned what healthy mourning looks like may never embark on healthy grief and mourning journeys. They end up, usually unwittingly, carrying their grief. This is often a longstanding complicated grief pattern in their lives, and they rarely associate their carried grief symptoms with past life losses.

But unembarked grief may also be a new phenomenon for any given griever. It's possible to have grieved and mourned in healthy ways in the past yet fail to launch on a new grief journey, especially when the circumstances of the recent death and the relationship with the person who died were especially challenging.

Delayed or postponed grief also falls into this category. Sometimes life circumstances force grievers to set aside their grief for a time to deal with seemingly more urgent matters, such as an illness or financial crisis. And sometimes grievers choose to postpone their grief by engaging in long-term denial or an avoidance pattern (see Off-trail grief, below) and telling themselves that they'll come to terms with their grief next month or after their child heads off to college in the fall or when they have more energy. "I'll think about it later," they often say. Deep down, many postponers hope that if they ignore their grief for a while, it will eventually just go away. Yet, as I have previously noted, grief waits on welcome, not on time.

Note that unembarked grief may present as absent grief—a self-proclaimed lack of painful thoughts and feelings, "feeling fine or normal," not suffering, i.e., unacknowledged grief—or it may present as absent mourning—experiencing profound and confusing pain inside but lacking the capacity, understanding, and/or support to convert that grief into external mourning. You may also see this as inhibited mourning, in which the griever speaks of the need to mourn but struggles to verbalize or otherwise express her thoughts and feelings about the loss, or minimized mourning, in which the griever is aware of feelings of grief but attempts to downplay or dilute them through a variety of rationalizations.

In fact, I have seen that intellectualizing grief is a common form of extended denial. These grievers often believe that grief is something to be quickly thought through but not felt through. Words become a substitute for authentic feeling. These minimizers seek to avoid pain at all cost. But as we have said, the journey through grief is primarily an emotional and spiritual journey. Intellectualizing is a type of non-starting. No matter how much the intellectualizer tries to explain things away, she is experiencing stuck-at-the-trailhead grief.

Impasse grief

Imagine you're hiking through the wilderness and on the trail, you come up against a sheer rock face or a massive downed tree. When you encounter such an obstruction, in order to proceed you must find a way through or around the obstruction, right?

Instead, people experiencing impasse grief remain stuck in that particular location. Not only can they not seem to get past the obstruction, they may not even recognize it as an obstruction. Rather, they may perceive that this struggle is simply what grief is like for them. They keep butting up against the same problem. It's as if the map of the wilderness of their grief is zoomed in on this one issue or feeling, and they've forgotten or never understood in the first place that the true boundaries of their grief journey are in fact broader and the terrain much more varied.

In my counseling experience, the obstruction often comes in the form of a pronounced and prolonged encounter with anger, anxiety, sadness, or guilt. To the griever, anger can seem like an active and just response, but even when the anger is understandable, it is a blocking force if it does not soften with time and mourning. Anxiety may take the form of panic attacks or chronic worry. Sadness, of course, often presents as clinical depression. And guilt can create an impasse because, the griever reasons, there is no going back and fixing things. There is only living with the guilt.

Other clinicians typically call this form of complicated grief "distorted grief," but I do not agree with the judgment cast by the term "distorted," meaning, as it does, something that is deformed, false, or perverted. The term "impasse grief" instead connotes the truth—that the mourning is not perverted or deformed but instead stuck on a particular feature. In the absence of concurrent mental illness, it's not that the feature itself is distorted. It's almost always a normal and necessary part of the landscape of the particular griever's journey.

Off-trail grief

Sometimes in that famous yellow wood where two roads diverge, grievers, usually unknowingly, take an unhelpful path. After all, it's not like there's a sign with two arrows, one saying "Healthy grief this way" and the other "Caution! Wrong way!" So they embark on or stumble onto a course that occupies them with other tasks and issues in lieu of their normal and necessary grief work. This course may even feel productive to them, because it gives them something *else* to focus on and do in the aftermath of their loss, but it's actually counterproductive. The path of their real grief starts back at that fork in the road where they veered off-course.

Off-trail grief behaviors are essentially avoidance patterns. They are habits and obsessions that replace the work of grief and mourning. Note that off-trail grief differs slightly from impasse grief because the latter contains a stuck, acute thought or feeling that is usually a normal and necessary part of the grief journey, while the former features a pronounced behavior that is often more tangential to the grief journey.

Also, I would be remiss here if I did not remind that some avoidance *is* normal and necessary in grief. As I have said, healthy mourning is a balance between evading and encountering. We cannot and should not try to live in the throes of our grief every moment of every day. (If we do, we are likely experiencing encamped grief. See page 122.) It's normal and necessary to authentically encounter our grief for a time then retreat to rest and rejuvenate. All of the avoidance behaviors listed below may be temporary means of survival and coping. It is when the patterns become fixed and pronounced, often displacing other healthy behaviors altogether, that I consider them off-trail grief.

Here are some of the most common off-trail mourning behaviors I have seen in my 40 years as a grief counselor and educator. Some grievers may primarily exhibit one of these patterns, while others may exhibit a combination.

Displacing

As you know, people in emotional and spiritual distress often take their feelings about one issue and project them onto another, usually because it feels safer or easier to channel the feelings in that direction. This happens in grief, too. For example, a griever may complain about troubles at work or relationships with others when the true source of the problem is unencountered, unmourned grief. I've also noticed that some grievers who avoid by displacing become bitter toward life in general, while others turn their bitterness inward, becoming full of self-hatred and possibly experiencing debilitating depression. When a griever who has experienced a significant loss, especially one replete with complicated grief risk factors, presents with emotional distress seemingly unrelated to the loss, displacement is likely the culprit. This avoidance pattern, which is almost always unconscious, is understandable and common.

Replacing

Grievers sometimes quickly move to replace the relationship that was severed by death. They prematurely reinvest the emotions that were part of the former relationship in a new relationship. Instead of mourning what was lost, they attempt to replace what was lost. This is a futile approach, however, because they cannot replace the person who died. Forming new relationships is healthy, of course, but only after a period of mourning and reconciliation. Grievers who replace are trying to do what society has so forcefully told them to do, which is "move on." They are typically unaware that their new relationship is a form of grief avoidance.

Somaticizing

The somaticizer feels his grief in the body, as physical symptoms, and turns his attention to these problems in lieu of his grief. It's important to note that physical symptoms such as fatigue, body aches, chest pains, nausea, sleeplessness, and others are quite normal in grief, and grievers should never be shamed for their physical symptoms. In fact, compassionate and attentive bodily self-care is essential to healing grief, and grievers who would benefit from help with their physical distress should also receive concurrent care from their medical practitioner.

But sometimes, physical problems in grief predominate to the extent that they overshadow every other normal and necessary symptom. The somaticizer may become so completely preoccupied with his physical challenges that he has little or no energy to relate to others and do the work of mourning.

The physical symptoms can range from relatively benign, minor complaints to serious illness. Occasionally somaticizing takes the form of experiencing, or worrying about experiencing, a physical illness that took the life of the person who died. Upon physical examination, there are often no organic findings.

Consider that somaticizers may be unconsciously adopting a "sick role" in order to be taken care of. When those around them (or grievers themselves) disenfranchise their legitimate need to grieve and mourn—and to be supported in their grief and mourning—they may turn to symptoms that will be taken seriously and that will get them the help they need.

"My husband was gardening when he died of a massive heart attack. I felt guilty that I had not found him sooner and gotten him help more quickly. I felt physically sick and kept going back to my doctor, but he couldn't find anything wrong with me. After working with my grief therapist for a while, I realized that I also needed to open up about an illegal abortion I'd had when I was 14. I hadn't told anyone about it—not even my husband. Talking about the abortion helped me feel better physically, and my guilt and grief over my husband's death got easier too."

Overworking

Another form of off-trail grief is overwork. After all, if you're putting in 10, 12, 15 hours a day on the job, you don't have time for anything else—including your painful thoughts and feelings. Interestingly, overworkers are often following the advice of well-wishers, who encourage them to "keep busy."

Of course, preexisting work addiction is a risk factor for this grief avoidance pattern. One man I saw in my practice found himself working 18 to 24 hours a day after the death of his wife. He literally worked himself to exhaustion every day. Through our work together, he came to understand that he was funneling all of his grief into his work. With support, he began to authentically encounter his grief. In other words, he returned to the fork in the road and set off down the healthy path.

Shopping

Some people rely on "retail therapy" when they're feeling stressed. As with all of the avoidance patterns we're discussing, a little of this behavior, for distraction and entertainment, is fine. As you know, the trouble comes when the behavior turns addictive and serves as a replacement for necessary emotional, social, and spiritual engagement. What's more, some shoppers get themselves into serious financial trouble as they spend beyond their means. Another form of this I have witnessed is the griever who, shortly after the death, begins giving away money with little discernment. This also frequently causes financial problems down the line.

Overeating

Have you ever companioned a griever who literally consumed his pain? In my experience, these grievers are unconsciously trying to fill the emptiness they feel inside them. We also know that stress can stimulate hunger centers in the brain.

Most of us turn to certain foods when we're craving the emotional high of endorphins—thus the term "comfort foods"—but some of us are more prone to overeating when we're feeling anxious or blue. People who overeat in grief may observe that they are gaining weight yet feel helpless to stop.

Substance abusing

Abusing alcohol or drugs is among the most dangerous of off-trail grief behaviors, yet grievers are often counseled by (and often joined by) well-intentioned friends and family members who recommend a few stiff drinks or liberal use of sleeping pills to quell their pain and knock them out. "Take this. It will make you feel better," they say.

On the contrary, we know that substance use often disrupts sleep patterns, worsens mood states, and increases agitation. What's more, it may become a significant destructive pattern of behavior that not only blocks the work of mourning for years to come but has many deleterious effects on the griever's life.

Other addictive behaviors

Shopping, eating, and substance abusing aren't the only addictive avoidance patterns in complicated grief, of course. In order to avoid their painful grief, grievers may turn to a wide range of compulsions, from gambling and sex to video games, internet surfing or porn, risk-taking, exercise, plastic surgery or other "self-improvement," and more. Essentially, any consuming behavior that thoroughly distracts them from their necessary grief and mourning puts them on the wrong path.

Traveling

Traveling grievers may literally stay on the move to avoid the work of mourning. It's like they're trying to outrun their grief. Our culture colludes with this misconception. People will often tell grievers, "What you need to do is get away, take a trip." Similarly, some grievers relocate prematurely. In an effort to make a clean break from their painful circumstances, they pack up and move.

But as Confucius said, "No matter where you go, there you are." What traveling grievers need help encountering is the reality that their grief lives inside them. What's more, early grief, especially, demands that grievers slow down and withdraw. Traveling, like overworking, is the opposite of this. And travelers and movers often find that they experience secondary losses as a result of their avoidance pattern, such as breaking from existing support systems, like family or church communities, and comforting routines. They may find themselves missing the very things they thought they were trying to escape.

Crusading

Crusading grievers convert their grief into over-dedication to or premature involvement with a cause. Often the cause is related to the circumstances of the death or the passions of the person who died. It's natural to want to get involved in Mothers Against Drunk Driving, for example, if your child was killed by a drunk driver. Other times grievers throw themselves into volunteering or leading a grief support group.

This behavior is often reinforced by others, who counsel that the combination of "staying busy" and helping others is the ticket to "getting over" grief. While supporting such causes is indeed worthwhile and can be a healthy part of the grief journey, I caution against too-early involvement and over-involvement. As with pretty much everything we're discussing in this book, it's a question of balance. Mourners at risk for complicated grief, especially, must give their unique grief the time and attention it deserves.

In my estimation, off-trail grief is so common as to be practically epidemic in our society today. Many people no longer understand or value the role of pain and suffering, so grievers find the idea of entering the true wilderness of grief distasteful if not anathema. Yet at the same time, it's hard to suppress grief altogether, and they can't help but experience painful thoughts and feelings, so they look for a powerful distraction. The playground of off-trail grief often seems like an attractive, compelling alternative.

Encamped grief

Sometimes on the journey through grief, people stop moving—forward, backward, or sideways—and instead step off the trail and set up permanent residence. They build themselves a shelter, unpack provisions, and settle in. These grievers are not so much stuck at a particular impasse as they are entrenched in the grief experience in general.

Others have called this complicated grief category "chronic grief." Its hallmark is unending, unchanging distress, usually but not always with depression. Chronic grievers are typically preoccupied with the person who died, choosing this preoccupation over nurturing relationships with living family and friends. They may also be obsessed with objects that belonged to the person who died, and are prone to depressive brooding. Essentially, encamped grievers attempt to keep the person who died alive, or their acute grief alive, under the misconception that if they really loved the person who died, they must maintain—even cherish—their intense grief.

Some encamped grievers begin to identify with their loss experience so strongly that they build their new self-identities around the death or the circumstances of the loss. Yes, you will sometimes witness a sense of pride, loyalty, or honor in the encamped griever. It's normal for grievers to be proud of and loyal to the person who died, but this feeling usually segues into complication when the pride, loyalty, and honor are overly entangled with the grief experience or the griever's new self-identity as a griever.

Regarding the belongings of the person who died, it's also normal for grievers to keep and be attached to linking objects, which are items that belonged to or are associated with the person who died.

Wearing a piece of the dead person's clothing, sleeping on the dead person's pillow or pillowcase, keeping special objects close at hand, displaying photos of the person who died—these and many other behaviors involving linking objects are normal. They offer comfort, they help grievers meet their mourning needs, and they help grievers transition to a new form of relationship with the person who died. These behaviors are not indicative of encamped grief but rather healthy mourning, which means they also soften over time as the griever experiences the divine momentum of active mourning.

Shrines, on the other hand, may be indicative of encamped grief. I want to be clear about the difference. In the griever's home, a display of photos and belongings of the person who died is not a shrine. A photo book in the griever's purse is not a shrine. But keeping the bedroom of the person who died exactly as it was, in the manner of a museum—unoccupied and unused—for years or decades after the death? That is a shrine. There is a line between engaging with memories of the person who died as well as maintaining a new form of relationship with the person who died and attempting to stop time or keep the person who died alive. Do you see the difference? Shrines tend to prevent grievers from continued momentum in grief. Instead, they are homages to grief and death.

I once was asked to provide a consultation to a husband who was very concerned about his wife. Their 27-year-old son had died eight years earlier, and the husband described his wife as essentially among the living dead. She was totally unavailable to him and her surviving adult children, chronically depressed, and rarely able to leave their home.

I arranged for a home visit when I was speaking in their area. The woman wanted to take me on a tour of their home so I could "get to know" her son. I discovered that every wall in every room was covered with photos of him. Even the garage held a gallery. A corner of the living room was occupied by a display case chockfull of linking objects. And in the master bedroom, affixed to the ceiling and positioned directly above her pillow, was a life-size poster of her son.

Obviously, this woman was experiencing encamped grief. Her intransigence in the wilderness of her grief was due in large part to the fact that she would not acknowledge, to herself or to anyone else, that her son had died by suicide. She insisted his death was a homicide and spent a great deal of time and energy trying to prove it. In the meantime, she kept her son alive by making her entire house, and her very life, a shrine to him. Her love for her son was beautiful, but she was not able to incorporate the death and the love into her continuing life. As she attempted to keep her dead son alive, she had become dead to herself and everyone around her. While I was able to refer her to an experienced grief counselor in her area of the country, she was never able to integrate her loss into her life. I understand her encamped grief continues to this day.

Taking inventory and creating a map

In the wilderness that is complicated grief, the features we have just reviewed are the most common symptoms and presentations I have encountered as, for 40 years, I have done the search-and-rescue work of understanding and helping complicated grievers.

You, too, will be looking for these symptoms and presentations as you begin to work with grievers who are new to you. You have probably been trained, as I was, to use the term "assessment" at this phase in the process, but it is a word I dislike. Like other medical-model semantics such as "diagnose" and "treat," the term "assess" implies that you are the expert of the griever's internal reality and he the neophyte, when in fact, the truth is the other way around.

When you break down the word "companion," you get "com" for "with" and "pan" for "bread." Someone you would share a meal with. A friend. An equal. Initially your job is to come to the table with a beginner's mind, curious and compassionate. You are there to learn about the griever's experience and listen to his story. Yes, you also bring knowledge about and experience with complicated grief to the table, but at least for the time being, these take a backseat to the unfolding of the griever's unique experiences and truths. You assume nothing. You judge nothing. You extrapolate nothing. Instead, you listen, and you learn. I hope you will keep this stance in mind in your first meetings with each griever.

In addition, I will reiterate that I do not believe in formulas to assess complicated grief. I simply do not believe that this symptom plus that symptom plus that symptom for this many months equals complicated grief. What's more, I don't believe in scales that purport to measure the intensity of a person's grief, such as the Subjective Units of Distress, or SUDS, scale. Grief, like love, is much more mysterious than that, and it defies numerical analysis.

So instead of assessing and measuring, let's talk about taking inventory of the complicated griever's present situation. This is something we don't do *to* the complicated griever but instead *with* the complicated griever. We ask them to help us understand not only what happened—how they got to this particular spot in this particular wilderness—but also what they are carrying.

Are they carrying sadness? If so, let's take a look at that sadness together. Are they carrying guilt? If so, let's take a look at that guilt together. What else? Memories. Other relationships. Concurrent life struggles. And what about strengths and assets? Memories might also appear in this part of the inventory, as might other relationships. Personality strengths. Faith. Life accomplishments. Hope for the future. It's important to remember that grief companioning is more assets-based than the medical model of grief care, which tends to be deficits-based.

I often don't like to talk about taking inventory with the griever until the end of the second or third session because until then, I'm not up to speed. With my beginner's mind and open heart, at first I'm still simply listening and learning. Only after the griever has let me know that she has finished summarizing her story and shared her most pressing symptoms and concerns are we ready to take a look at the inventory and map together.

I am often asked by bereavement caregivers to provide grief checklists. Many therapists would like simple assessment forms or checklists as well as a treatment plan form so they can easily check boxes and start stepping through topics and techniques with the griever. I don't like these forms because too often they are reductive and hurry-up-and-fix-it oriented. In the Complicated Grief Educational Supplement, however, I have provided an **Inventory form 28** that can be used to note grievers' loss circumstances, complicated grief risk factors, symptoms, strengths, challenges, and goals. This is a worksheet that is intended to be filled out together with the griever and sent home with the griever (though you'll want to keep a copy for your files, of course). There is also a **Mourning Map form 30** that, in combination with the content of Part Three, captures on paper potential mourning work ideas *as they some up session by session.* The Mourning Map is also meant to be written with the griever, but it will not be completed all at once but rather as opportunities, insights, and divine momentum occur. Both the Inventory and Mourning Map should be as transparent and griever-led as possible. They are tools for the griever as much as they are for you. They are also tentative and adaptable instead of cemented-in-place. As symptoms soften or change and new challenges and successes arise, they should be amended, added to, or recreated.

So far in this book we have discussed how the terrain of grief becomes so complicated sometimes and the ways in which the griever typically responds to that terrain. We've reviewed the typical features of the topography, and we've covered the signs to look for in determining who needs help.

Once we've met the stuck or lost griever where he is in his wilderness and we've taken the time to understand the unique terrain of his grief, it's our role, responsibility, and privilege to help him return to the path that leads to healing. In other words, we've searched and found, and now it's time to rescue. But…*how* do we do that? What do we do (and not do) to help him get unlost and unstuck? That is the subject of Part Three.

Questions for reflection and understanding

In a blank notebook or computer file, I invite you to answer the provided questions below. Writing down your thoughts will help you understand and remember the concepts as well as integrate them with your unique methods of helping grievers.

Which care-eliciting symptoms have I commonly seen in complicated grievers?

Which care-eliciting symptoms have I seen but less frequently in complicated grievers?

For each of the following care-eliciting grief symptoms, please make note of any questions or comments you may have.

Shock, numbness, denial, and disbelief

Disorganization, confusion, searching, and yearning

Griefbursts

Anxiety, panic, and fear

Explosive emotions

Dirty pain

Guilt, regret, and self-blame

Sadness and depression

Carried grief symptoms

    Difficulties with trust and intimacy

    Depression and negative outlook

    Anxiety and panic attacks

    Psychic numbing and disconnection

    Irritability and agitation

    Substance abuse, addictions, eating disorders

    Physical problems, real or imagined

For each of the following complicated grief categories, please make note of any questions or comments you may have.

Unembarked grief

Impasse grief

Off-trail grief

    Displacing

    Replacing

    Somaticizing

    Overworking

    Shopping

    Overeating

    Substance abusing

    Other addictive behaviors

    Traveling

    Crusading

Encamped grief

Other thoughts or questions related to Part Two

PART THREE

Companioning People Experiencing Complicated Grief

A 37-year-old farmer—let's call him Robert—was referred to me by a psychiatrist who was seeing Robert and his wife, Mary, in couple's therapy. Robert and Mary had been married for four years and were struggling in their relationship. Mary was Robert's second wife. His first marriage, to Sally, had lasted 12 years then ended abruptly when Sally died in a farming accident.

As was their routine, Sally and Robert had been working side-by-side in the fields. Robert was driving the tractor; Sally was riding on the tractor. Sally fell from the tractor and suffered massive internal injuries from a piece of equipment being pulled behind the tractor. Robert married Mary nine months later.

The psychiatrist suspected that the true source of Robert and Mary's marital problems was his unreconciled grief over the death of Sally. Understandably, Robert continued to grieve inside, struggling with feelings of loss as well as guilt over the circumstances of the death. He and Sally had been extremely close, spending the bulk of every day together. Their close relationship naturally heightened his grief. What's more, Robert tended to suppress his emotions, partly due to family-of-origin "rules" around stoicism in the face of death and grief and partly due to a perceived need to protect Mary from his ongoing feelings about Sally. And finally, his off-trail grief path of replacing his dead wife prematurely further complicated his already complicated journey.

So what do we as grief companions do when we find such a griever in the wilderness? Clearly he was lost and struggling. Surely his future happiness and fulfillment were at stake. But it's absolutely essential to understand that as grief companions, it is not our job to call in a helicopter and have complicated grievers airlifted out. Instead, it is our responsibility to meet up with and stay with them to help them safely traverse the most challenging leg of their journey. After all, there is no going around this wilderness or giving up and returning to the trailhead. There is only going through it.

In this section we will be having a conversation about how to walk alongside and companion complicated grievers right where they are—in the most harrowing sections of their unique wildernesses. Before we begin, I want to reiterate a few foundational principles:

• All grief is normal and necessary.

• All grief is complicated and unique.

• For a variety of reasons, some people experience extra-complicated grief. That is the subject of this book, though we have agreed to simply call it "complicated grief."

• Any number and combination of extraordinary loss circumstances and risk factors may give rise to complicated grief.

• Circumstances and risk factors need not seem extraordinary, at least from the outside, to create significant complications for grievers.

• The care-eliciting symptoms of complicated grief are the same as normal grief symptoms and may only differ in degree, feature prominence, functional impact, and, sometimes, duration.

• In determining where to draw the line between normal grief and complicated grief, the most important question is: Would this griever likely benefit from compassionate professional companionship?

Now is also a good time to review the Tenets of Companioning in the Introduction, which you'll find on page 10. These are the other foundational principles that undergird the companioning model we'll review in this section. To reiterate, companioning is about presence, learning, and bearing witness to what is fundamentally a spiritual or soul-based journey. As I also said in the Introduction, it is not the grief companion's role to carry, lead, or find the way out of the wilderness, but it is our responsibility to check and safeguard vital signs, provide shelter, offer sustenance, and carry a toolkit. We are not rescuers in the saver or savior sense; rather, we are rescuers in the "thank goodness you're here to help me" sense.

Now let's do some rescuing.

Checking and safeguarding vital signs

What's the first thing you do when you approach a compromised hiker in the wilderness? You check to make sure his vitals are OK. Heartbeat? Check. Breathing? Check. Body temperature? Check. Blood pressure? Check. Hydration? Check.

To check and safeguard the griever's vital signs, in addition to **basic physical wellness** you will be looking for **signs of suicidal ideation, clinical depression, panic attacks, post-traumatic stress, or other immediate and possibly life-threatening co-occurring mental-health challenges.** Don't forget also to note any basic **vital signs that are strong**. What assets does the griever have in her favor?

You are trained to make such initial and ongoing assessments and treat and refer clients accordingly. Sometimes you will have to refer a complicated griever for vital-sign care (such as addiction treatment) before she can return to your companionship. Sometimes you may be able to companion concurrently with treatment for acute health issues. I urge you to exercise your best professional judgment and never hesitate to seek a second opinion and/or mentorship whenever you are unsure. Grief companionship is essential for complicated grievers, but unless and until **basic health and safety issues** are addressed, renewed momentum in the grief journey cannot be realized.

Providing shelter

When you first meet a griever in his wilderness, **establishing safety** is the critical first step. The griever must feel safe, both in his life and in your care. After vital-sign stability is ensured, grief companions further a sense of safety with **trust** and **hospitality.**

Trust is about consistency and safety. Complicated grief often naturally leaves grievers feeling a lack of trust in the world around them. They often question, knowingly or unknowingly, if they should risk trusting again. As a companion, you have an obligation to establish a strong sense of trust in the first few sessions then continue to safeguard that trust. Complicated grievers must feel consistently safe in your office or they will be unable to engage in the hard, heroic work of mourning. Any attempt to invite them to go deeply or actively mourn before they feel safe with you may well end in them feeling violated and shutting down. Remember—go slow. There are no rewards for speed! The good news is that when trust does develop between you and the griever, there is a palpable exchange of energy. Conversely, when trust is lacking or absent, no energy is exchanged and nothing happens.

Hospitality is the essence of knowing how to live in society. Among the ancient Greeks, hospitality was a necessary element of day-to-day life. In a land where borders were permeable, it was important to get to know one's neighbors as potential friends.

One way to do this was to share meals together. First, the guest and host would pour a libation to the gods. Then they would eat ("break bread") together. Then, after the guest had his fill, they would tell each other their stories, with the guest going first. Often, tears were shed because their stories were highly personal; battles, family, histories, and life tragedies were recounted. After the evening together, the host and guest were potential allies. Still today, breaking bread and sharing personal stories are key elements of companioning people through death and grief.

The spiritual thinker Henri Nouwen once elegantly described hospitality as the "creation of a free space where the stranger can enter and become a friend instead of an enemy." He observed that hospitality is not about trying to change people, but instead about offering them space where change can take place. He astutely noted, "Hospitality is not a subtle invitation to adopt the lifestyle of the host, but the gift of a chance for the guest to find his own."

In the wilderness of complicated grief, grief companions provide hospitality by establishing a safe harbor with empathy and effective basic counseling skills. The griever must understand that you are trained and competent but also empathetic, trustworthy, genuine, engaged, and hopeful. You are there to support but not save. You are there to listen, learn, and bear witness before offering any guidance.

I also recommend **educating** the grievers in your care about normal grief, complicated grief, mourning needs, and goals of your time together as part of providing shelter. That is why I created the Complicated Grief Educational Supplement. While it is true that grief is primarily a spiritual, soul-based journey and that grief companioning is more art than science, more heart than head, the grievers we care for deserve to know our underlying assumptions and rationales. Understandably, grievers are often anxious about talk therapy procedures and process. They want to know what is considered "normal" and what they can expect from the sessions. In my experience, it is both respectful and calming to the griever to take some time in the first few sessions to briefly review your foundational beliefs about grief and methods of work. As sessions continue, it is also appropriate to restate a principle whenever the griever is in need of affirmation.

Offering sustenance

In the wilderness of complicated grief, grievers are often depleted of energy. They are often starved of support. A precondition to help another human being integrate loss into her life is to create a "holding environment" anchored in empathy, immediacy, hope, and heart.

Empathy is the art of bearing witness and, as you do so, exuding acceptance, compassion, and warmth. It is about allowing the griever to teach you instead of the other way around. As a companion, you do not judge or prescribe. Rather, you seek to understand each unique griever's story and convey a warm, accepting presence.

Immediacy is also of critical importance when companioning fellow humans through complications of grief. In our distracted, media-addicted world, immediacy is about being fully and completely present to the mourner in the here and now. It goes beyond the content of what is being said to the process of what is happening from moment to moment. The griever's needs are right there in the present moment, and immediacy allows you to be empathetically responsive to those needs. After all, the present moment is where the needs of the soul reside, and grief work, particularly complicated grief work, is anchored in soul work.

In addition to empathy and immediacy, effective grief companions provide the sustenance of **hope**, which is an expectation of a good that is yet to be. It is an expression of the present alive with a sense of the possible. It is through your genuine sense of hope that you communicate your belief that the mourner can and will heal, or "become whole again." In my work companioning complicated grievers, I often think of hope as similar to an IV in intensive care—it's constantly but unobtrusively working to ensure a slow but steady drip-drip-drip infusion of expectancy and optimism.

While the quality of hopefulness in a grief companion is about as easy to pin down as Jell-o, we all know it when we experience it in someone else. If you are genuinely, deep-down hopeful, you will not be able to help but communicate your hopefulness to mourners through all of your helping skills. Your body language will be hopeful. Your tone will be hopeful. This is definitely not to say that you should act overly cheerful or gloss over pain. No, you are never there to "buck up" complicated grievers. You must be willing and able to be present to profound pain, sometimes for long stretches of time, and believe in the necessity of sitting in the wound of grief. Yet, even as you are joining the griever in her pain, you are present to her with the deep knowing that the pain is creating movement toward meaning and purpose. I use the term "perturbation" to refer to this capacity to experience change and movement. To integrate grief requires that the griever be touched by what she is experiencing. If she does not allow herself (or is not allowed by others) to be touched, she cannot incorporate her grief into a new self and she cannot begin to live her changed life forward. Instead, she gets stuck or veers off-trail.

You use your companioning skills to help her, over time, fully explore and express her pain because you wholeheartedly believe in the transformative power of grief work.

Finally, to have **heart** as you companion people in complicated grief is to be true to your own feelings, humanness, and vulnerabilities. When you work from a place of heart, you function as a whole. When you are analytical, on the other hand, the thinking self is in charge. Being a true companion naturally occurs when you relax into yourself and bring compassion to all of your helping efforts. When you minister from your heart, you are in a state of deep connection with the divine, with yourself, and with your fellow human beings.

Carrying a toolkit

You come to this book with training and experience in mental-health care. It is likely that you already use and feel comfortable with certain methodologies and techniques. Whatever your current toolkit and therapeutic orientation, I believe that **griever-centered talk therapy** is the bedrock of companioning complicated grievers.

First of all, what do I mean by "griever-centered?" I mean that the griever and his highest-priority thoughts and feelings should guide every session. Rather than follow a prescribed sequential session plan, it's essential to let the griever choose at every fork in the road. What is most heavy and pressing on his mind and heart on any given day—or most welcome and in need of expression, such as new insights and gratitudes—should take precedence at any given session.

One exception to this principle often comes into play when grievers have experienced multiple losses. Loss-overloaded grievers usually need help getting started and more guidance or direction along the way. Another exception is for grievers who are stuck in denial or avoidance. In such cases, you must judiciously employ the art of supportive confrontation, pointing the unembarked, impassed, or off-trail griever to the effective path and then stepping back and allowing him to lead you there.

Second, talk therapy comes in a variety of flavors. Cognitive behavioral therapy (CBT), dialectic behavior therapy (DBT), interpersonal therapy (IPT), narrative therapy, and classic psychotherapy are some of the main types in use today. Many mental-health caregivers, perhaps including you, use a combination of these techniques in working with the people in their care.

If you are trained in employing various types of talk therapy, by all means, keep them in your toolkit and draw upon them when you think they will help. But I also think that therapeutic techniques can often be tossed out the window in favor of good old-fashioned listening. Remember—the complicated griever is not ill. He does not need treatment or a "cure." While he is stuck or off-trail in a tricky predicament, what he may need most is simply to express his inner thoughts and feelings as they arise and change over time. Talking them through in the presence of someone who deeply listens, accepts, and affirms, week after week, will help return him to a healthy path.

Of course, good old-fashioned listening all by itself is insufficient to help complicated grievers. Make no mistake: This is not beginner-level work. But when the listening ears and heart are attached to a trained, compassionate professional such as yourself—someone who has been formally educated but has also internalized the mysterious body of knowledge surrounding loss and grief, someone who knows how and when to appropriately dose grievers with the six needs of mourning—empathetic, self-as-instrument listening becomes the centerpiece tool in the toolkit.

Grief counseling versus grief therapy

Here at my Center for Loss and Life Transition, I teach a number of training classes for bereavement caregivers each year. A wide variety of professionals and laypeople attend, from psychiatrists and clinical therapists to clergy, hospice caregivers, church support group leaders, funeral home aftercare staff, and more. I believe that with training, all of them have the capacity to support their fellow human beings through the journey we call grief.

Complicated grief, however, is a more challenging form of grief that usually requires the companionship of not only a professional mental-health caregiver, but one with specific training, experience, and interest in grief therapy. Please consider the following distinctions between grief counseling and grief therapy as you decide whether you are adequately trained and experienced to support any given griever.

Grief counseling	Grief therapy
Educative	Reconstructive
Supportive	Depth emphasis
Situational	Interpretive
Focus on present	Focus on both present and past
Emphasis on normalcy	Emphasis on complications

As a grief companion, one of your most important tools is an understanding of when to choose to work with a griever and when to refer. All grief companions must be good at listening, understanding, educating, supporting, advocating, and encouraging, but especially when it comes to complicated grief, referring skills and discernment top the list.

I've emphasized that it's often difficult to clearly label an individual's grief as either "complicated" or "normal." This can make the keep-or-refer decision especially tricky. Whenever you're in doubt, I urge you to seek the counsel and mentorship of other caregivers in your network. In addition, some of you have no desire to be therapists. That's OK! The information in this book will help you know when to refer. We need great grief counselors, and we also need great referrers. Finally, if your current skills fall primarily in the left column but you enjoy companioning grievers, I hope you'll look into acquiring additional training and certification. There are not enough grief companion therapists out there to fill the need, and we would welcome you to the fold.

Curing versus caring

"Cure" means to eradicate an illness. As we have emphasized throughout this book, grief is not an illness. Care, on the other hand, is being present to, bearing witness to, suffering with, and feeling with. Cure also means "to change." Caregivers often want to bring about change in people's lives, but cure can potentially damage if it does not grow out of care. Care is anchored in compassion and service and recognizes that this person who is hurting is my fellow human being, my brother or sister, mortal and vulnerable. And grief can never be eradicated, "gotten over," or "recovered from." It can only be experienced, and, through active engagement and movement, reconciled. Caring is about witnessing grief; curing is about discouraging it. Caring is anchored in service; curing is anchored in fixing. We grief companions are caregivers, not curegivers.

Self as instrument

In the mid-1900s, humanist thinker and educational theorist Arthur Wright Combs proposed a helping concept he called "self as instrument." By this he meant that teachers and other helpers and caregivers are not simply indistinguishable technicians who deliver services mechanically or uniformly. Rather, they are unique individuals who use their whole selves to shape and funnel the care or services they provide. Not only are their methods unique, their interactions are also highly tailored to the needs and personalities of each unique person in their care.

Caregivers who see themselves as instruments in their work are creative, adaptable, and passionate. Grief companions with the self-as-instrument mindset are congruently suited to the role. Their inner beliefs and passions align strongly with the companioning philosophy. Their personalities as well as innate strengths and weaknesses make them good listeners and helpers. They also often have life experiences that have sensitized them to loss and grief and the importance of compassionate grief support.

I believe that complicated grievers, especially, need grief companions who embrace the self-as-instrument philosophy. To me, companioning grievers is a calling and spiritual ministry.

Mourning as "treatment" ㉙

Foundational to my philosophy of and professional experience in grief care is that the only effective way to "treat" complicated grief is with mourning, which is the outward expression of grief. Mourning is normal and necessary, but it is often part of the stuckness in the wilderness of complicated grief. Whenever grief is naturally complex, the griever's need to mourn and means of effective mourning also become more complex. The risk for complicated mourning—or grief expressions that are impassed, off-trail, or encamped—also rises.

I invite you to think of the mourning required of complicated grief as akin to summiting Mount Everest. That isn't the case for the mourning needed for normal grief. You and I can go for a day hike in the relatively low-altitude mountain foothills outside my home in Colorado at any time. We can head out for an hour or two and easily walk the well-groomed paths. We don't need any special equipment or experience. We don't need to carry oxygen. We don't need the help of a professional guide. But with complicated grief, the terrain is more difficult and dangerous, and once it is impassed, off-trail, or encamped (or sometimes unembarked on altogether), the mourning needed to traverse the harrowing topography also becomes more challenging.

A couple of years ago I crafted a new theory of mourning for soulmates whose partners had died. What I had learned over several decades from this unique set of grievers was that their devastation over the loss of their soulmate was deeper and wider and more all-encompassing than any other grief they had ever experienced in their lives. Because their attachment was profound, their grief was profound. In other words, it was complicated. It was complicated by the unparalleled nature of the relationship. And furthermore, they taught me, the resources out there to help them with their grief felt inadequate. They sought grief support that affirmed their unique loss and was commensurate with its severity.

So, in an effort to help grieving soulmates, I proposed a theory of healing I called "heroic mourning." While I believe that grief is always deeply challenging and painful and thus all mourning is heroic, I realized that the naturally complicated and outsized grief of soulmates required equally epic mourning. To create continued momentum in their grief journeys, I suggested, grieving soulmates had to mourn as grandly as they had loved. I offered this theory in my book *When Your Soulmate Dies*, which I have already mentioned. I'm happy to report that thousands of soulmates have since read the book and, based on the reviews, found it a helpful way to think about their uniquely challenging quests to heal.

Soon it came time for me to work on this book on complicated grief. It didn't take long for me to connect the dots. Right away I realized that all forms of complicated grief require heroic mourning. Whenever the terrain of the grief wilderness is particularly harrowing, as it is with soulmate loss but also losses associated with all the risk factors we reviewed in Part One, it's just plain harder to navigate. The peaks are higher and the valleys lower. The trail is rockier and riddled with menacing predators and outsized hurdles. Simply to keep going on this trail is not for the faint of heart. It requires extra heroism and fortitude. Please keep this idea of heroic mourning in mind as you read the remainder of Part Three and companion the complicated grievers in your care.

An overview of the companioning model for complicated grief

As we have said, complicated grievers are essentially stuck or off-trail in the especially complex terrain of the wilderness of their grief. They need help returning to a healthy path and starting to move again. They need help regrouping and re-embarking. They need help catching up so that they can realize the lifelong, life-giving benefits of divine momentum and reconciliation.

Some years ago I created a basic four-step model for grievers to work through unembarked (or carried) grief, but in fact this model applies to all types and presentations of complicated grief. An awareness of the four steps can assist you in your work with complicated grievers because you will know to anticipate each of the steps, affirm them as normal and necessary, and find ways to help grievers work through each of them.

The steps for complicated grief work are as follows:

1. IDENTIFYING AND ACKNOWLEDGING THE COMPLICATED GRIEF

In your first sessions together, you will allow the griever to teach you about her unique history, life, challenges, strengths, and stories of loss. With a beginner's mind, you will listen and you will learn. Of course, you will also bring your professional complicated grief knowledge (about such things as risk factors and symptoms) as well as clinical experience to these sessions, but you will remain open and humble, setting aside the counterproductive constructs of "expert" and "patient" and instead donning the mantle of companion and fellow human being.

As grievers share, you will be listening and affirming with high levels of empathy. You will exercise non-judgment and exude the assumption that grievers have been doing the best they could in coping with their grief. I sometimes say that aloud to grievers: "You have been doing the very best you knew how to do with your extra-complicated grief and loss circumstances. I am honored to companion you as we find ways for you to do the healing work of mourning. I am here to help you do that work." You will be reminding the griever that you are in this together and that you are committed to helping her reignite hope and create divine momentum toward healing.

During this discovery process, you and the grievers together will begin to identify and acknowledge their complicated grief. When you meet them where they are in the wilderness, some grievers will be more aware of their predicament than others. In other words, the initial degree of acknowledgment that they are stuck and need help will vary. However, my professional experience has taught me that while many people with complicated grief do not seek therapy, those who do are often amenable to the work that must be done to restore their divine sparks. In other words, most complicated grievers who find their way to your care will be ready to identify and acknowledge.

In my professional experience with complicated grievers, it typically takes a minimum of three sessions to explore and reach solid identification and understanding. Toward the end of this phase, it is appropriate to offer gentle education to grievers about grief and complicated grief. While you are not the expert of the grievers' grief—they are—you do have general information that will help them understand the grief process and the need for mourning. You also can help dispel any misconceptions they might well harbor about grief and mourning. They will teach you about their grief, and in small doses and with appropriate timing, you will teach them about grief in general. You will also name and review their particular grief complications. You might say, for example, "You have suffered so many losses in such a short period of time that it makes sense that you feel you are drowning in your grief. You are experiencing loss overload. It's normal for people in your situation to struggle. Together we will create a plan to help you through this." As you educate, you will simultaneously be providing hope and normalizing grievers' experiences.

I sometimes use the analogy of intensive care with complicated grievers. Just as people with serious injuries require special care and attention in the ICU, grievers with unusually severe loss injuries also require special care and attention. That is what we are there to provide.

2. OVERCOMING RESISTANCE TO DO THE GRIEF WORK REQUIRED

While complicated grievers who do seek help are usually open to the therapy in general, it is common for them to resist encountering certain aspects of their grief and expressing it outside themselves in the ways you will suggest. This is normal. After all, grief is hard, and complicated grief is harder. Who would choose to experience that degree of pain?

Some grievers fear that if they start really focusing on and expressing their deepest thoughts and feelings, they'll never be able to stop. Others are afraid of revealing what they feel inside because they worry they're "not normal" or "going crazy." Again, this is another call for the companion to create a holding environment anchored in trust, hospitality, empathy, immediacy, hope, and heart.

Your companioning role in this step is to normalize and exude hope. Assure grievers that while it is natural to resist encountering painful grief and doing the work of mourning, it is an essential and ultimately momentum-giving step on their journey. Obviously, this seems counterintuitive to many people in grief, so be patient in helping them understand this essential truth.

Grief and mourning are actually their friend and the natural consequence of having loved. You are there to walk alongside them as they do the hardest work, and together you will get through it. Be sure to relate to them that as with many perceived hurdles in life, the anticipation is often worse than the reality. Complicated grievers who are avoiding certain mourning needs (which we'll discuss next) typically remark, after guided encounters with those needs, "That wasn't as bad as I thought it was going to be." What a privilege to companion—not treat!—fellow human beings in befriending this process!

3. ACTIVELY MOURNING THE COMPLICATED GRIEF

We'll be talking about the griever's six central needs of mourning next, but for now it suffices to say that grief therapy works because it provides a supportive environment and structure in which grievers are encouraged to actively encounter and express their grief.

Yes, active mourning is the key to reconciling all grief, including complicated grief. It is not just the main thing; it is the only thing. It is the companion's job to facilitate active mourning, offer empathy related to the distress, and affirm all the while that the painful encounters will lead to healing. As you help facilitate this process, you remember to project a quiet humility, not an arrogant expertise. And humility interfaces with developing a service ethic—genuinely wanting to care for others while at the same time realizing you are not in charge. Instead, you submit yourself to the tenets of companioning and open your soul to the mysterious journey of complicated grief.

4. INTEGRATING THE COMPLICATED GRIEF

Integrating complicated grief essentially means getting back on a healthy path to healing. It entails getting unstuck and from there forward, incorporating the new approach to grief, mourning, and healing learned in therapy.

We'll be reviewing the overall goal of reconciliation later in this section. It is important to remember that with complicated grief, the companion's role is primarily to accompany the griever through the roughest patch, ensuring a return to (or start on) healthy footing and good momentum. You hope to have the privilege of companioning complicated grievers all the way through integration and reconciliation. The integration of the complications and care-eliciting symptoms are at the heart of the complicated griever's steepest challenges and must be your focus and your mission. But with you at their side, the complicated grievers in your care are never alone, never truly lost, and always in sight of hope!

You will rely on the four steps of the companioning model throughout all of your sessions with each complicated griever. While the steps are not really sequential and in fact overlap all the time, it is true that you will facilitate more work on the first two steps in the beginning of your time with the griever, moving to focus on the second steps in your later sessions. Still, because grief is recursive, you will also find that on any given day, the griever may again need help re-acknowledging the reality of his complicated grief and/or overcoming resistance to do the work. Active mourning will likely take place at every session, though you should see a general, overall trend of softening of symptoms as you continue to meet. And some signs of integration may already be in place when you first start seeing a griever. He may, for example, have some awareness of personal growth that he has already experienced since the death. In other words, he may have made progress in some areas and be stuck in others.

As you help the griever move through the four steps (non-sequentially and recursively), be sure to expressly affirm each accomplishment. You might say at the end of a session, "You have focused on work that needed your attention. It's so very hard to befriend the most painful parts of your grief, but you are doing the necessary work." Appropriately acknowledging and celebrating every bit of progress is a critical part of the companion's role. I often think of this as acknowledging the divine momentum that is now taking place—reinforcing the hope is essential to the integration of grief.

And now it's time to dive deeper into the "how" of companioning people experiencing complicated grief. If the four-step model of companioning complicated grievers is the overall, high-level process, the six needs of mourning are the mid-level framework. They are the must-stop waystations on the journey, and facilitating grievers' encounters with them is your main role as grief companion.

The six needs of mourning ㉙

As previously noted, the reality is that active mourning is the key to reconciling grief, and the topic we are about to discuss—the six needs of mourning—are the key to active mourning. They are the heart of the therapeutic process with grievers, complicated and uncomplicated. Through my formal training and, more important, my four decades of experience as a grief companion, I have learned that if they are to experience movement in their grief journeys and find their way to eventual reconciliation, all grievers have six central needs that they must engage with and continue to meet as the needs arise and re-arise over time.

Mourning Need 1:   Acknowledge the reality of the death

Mourning Need 2:   Embrace the pain of the loss

Mourning Need 3:   Remember the person who died

Mourning Need 4:   Develop a new self-identity

Mourning Need 5:   Search for meaning

Mourning Need 6:   Receive and accept ongoing support from others

In other words, the six needs are the keys to ongoing momentum in grief. They are, if you will, both the path and the fuel for the journey. And since we have agreed that complicated grief is grief that has gotten stuck or off-trail somewhere along the way, helping the griever regain healthy momentum through judicious, griever-led dosing with the six needs is the grief companion's most effective model.

In the four-step complicated grief companioning model we reviewed starting on page 142, the six needs of mourning come into play under step three: active mourning. Step three is the focused, engaged grief work that you will facilitate while the griever is in your care, and the six needs are essentially the how-tos of this grief work.

A brief history of "grief work"

Before we dive into the details, I would be remiss if I did not point out that my six needs of mourning build on and relate to concepts put forth in past decades by the bereavement luminaries you and I both learned from along the way. As you are well aware, there are many ways of describing the grief process, and many different perspectives and theories that undergird these descriptions. While it was Freud who first introduced the concept of the active steps required in grief, it was the psychiatrist Dr. Erich Lindemann who in 1944 coined the term "grief work" to describe the griever's essential tasks and processes. He believed these were, in his words, emancipation from bondage to the deceased, readjustment to a world without the deceased, and the formation of new relationships. In the 1970s, Dr. John Bowlby and his colleague Dr. Colin Murray Parkes described four phases of grief: shock and numbness, yearning and searching, despair and disorganization, and reorganization and recovery. Since then, many others have weighed in on the concept of grief as a series of discrete tasks or steps, including Elisabeth Kübler-Ross, whose 1969 "stages of grief" so captured (and still holds, albeit usually inaccurately) the world's attention. We owe her a debt for her theory because it provided the impetus for a more open discussion about death in our grief-avoidant culture.

In 1992, Dr. William J. Worden, a founding member of the Association of Death Education and Counseling, proposed a model of four tasks of mourning (which you will recognize as somewhat similar to my six-needs model): accept the reality of the loss; process the pain of grief; adjust to a world without the person who died; and find an enduring connection with the person who died while also embarking on a new life. I also appreciate the contributions of my colleague Dr. Therese Rando, who in 1993 proposed the six "R" processes of mourning listed on page 20.

More recently, Drs. Margaret Stroebe and Henk Schut's 1999 "dual-process" model described the action of grief as a vacillation between engaging with the inner emotions and dealing with the outside world, including taking care of practical matters caused by the death and engaging in activities that help the griever escape. I call the griever's natural and necessary see-saw-like need to approach his grief then step away, approach then step away, "evade-encounter," and I'll be touching on it in this section.

In this century there has been a move away from the idea of rigid tasks or stages and toward the understanding that each person's grief as well as mourning needs are completely unique—one-of-a-kind, like a snowflake or fingerprint. In general, this is an excellent development because it takes a step back from the medical model and puts expertise and ownership of grief where it belongs—with the griever.

Still, while I absolutely agree that each person's grief journey is unique, we as companions also see patterns of responses and needs, of course, among the grievers in our care, and these commonalities help us both affirm the griever's normalcy, even when the grief is extra complicated, and provide a framework for helping. That's what the six needs of mourning are—a framework and part of our toolkit.

Essentially, I am guided in my work with complicated grievers by the relationship between their symptoms and the six needs of mourning. As they teach me about their unique stories and symptoms, I listen for the link between their symptoms and an inhibition of one or more of the six needs. They know what they are feeling and experiencing. I know that they have core mourning needs that are not being met. My helping role is to connect the two and provide a safe space and compassionate presence in which the griever can begin to meet those unmet mourning needs—a process that will then, slowly and over time, begin to ease their symptoms. While there remains some controversy around the concept of "grief work"—because of its earlier association with the

WHEN GRIEF IS COMPLICATED

inaccurate and harmful idea that grievers must eventually "let go" or "resolve" their grief, as well as, on the other end of the spectrum, the newer proposal that grief work is just plain unnecessary (see "The new science of grief," page 204)—my professional experience has affirmed that it is active engagement with the six needs of mourning that helps grievers heal. Yes, the six needs are work. There is indeed grief work that needs doing.

In your work with complicated grievers, you will find, as I have, that people experiencing complicated grief are essentially stalled on one or more of the six needs of mourning. Their symptoms, presentations, and stories help us as companions discern which one or more of the six needs they need help encountering at any given time. It is then our job as companions to help "dose" the griever with the mourning need(s) that correspond to their symptom-specific, unembarked, impassed, off-trail, or encamped grief.

If you are a beginner therapist or new to the concept of companioning, it will likely take you some time and practice to be able to identify and interpret the symptoms the griever is shining the light on and correlate them to the mourning needs. In fact, I have often thought of my role as detective, because symptoms are often complex and often mask other hidden issues and because tying any particular symptom to a mourning need is not always straightforward. As you learn, I urge you to be compassionate and go slowly. There are no rewards for speed.

You will also find that active engagement with the six needs of mourning looks different from griever to griever, and that's OK. We've said that emotionality, for example, varies from person to person. Not every griever needs to process feelings by weeping or growing distraught. As long as a griever is authentically and fully expressing her unique inner thoughts and feelings in her unique way, she is doing her grief work.

Please note that the six needs apply to both normal grief and complicated grief, but as I suggested above, each need is made more naturally complicated in complicated grief. In other words, it is typically more challenging and difficult for the complicated griever to meet some or all of the needs, and mourning in ways that fully meet each need is also more challenging. The mourning required of complicated grief almost always takes longer and requires more heightened expression than in normal grief. Remember the idea of heroic mourning we talked about on page 141? This is where that concept comes into play.

Also note that though I've numbered them one through six, the mourning needs are not sequential in real life, nor are they items on a checklist. It's more common than not for grievers to be working on more than one need at a time. What's more, any given need will typically come and go in different amplitudes and guises, recurring for months and, especially in the cases of complicated grief, years.

Facilitating grievers' therapeutic work on the six needs of mourning

Now let's explore the six needs of mourning, the grief symptoms that may indicate an inhibition of each need, and my therapeutic suggestions and recommendations to facilitate grievers' necessary encounters with each need.

MOURNING NEED 1: ACKNOWLEDGE THE REALITY OF THE DEATH

The griever must confront and acknowledge, cognitively and emotionally, the reality that someone he loves will never be physically present in his life again. Whether the death was sudden or anticipated, acknowledging the full reality may take months or even years. As humans, we can know something in our heads (the cognitive reality) but not in our hearts (the affective reality).

In complicated grief, this need is often under-met in situations in which the circumstances of the death are particularly hard to fathom (such as homicide, suicide, or when the body is irrecoverable), there was hyper-dependence in the relationship, a funeral was not held or the body not viewed, or cultural, religious, or family systems influences shut down open discussion of the death.

What's more, in cases of complicated grief, it is common for grievers to acknowledge some of the realities of the death but not *all* realities of the death. Grievers may acknowledge the fact that their loved one is dead, for example, but they may not fully acknowledge the cause of the death or some of the circumstances related to the death. Earlier I mentioned an example of a woman whose grief was encamped because she focused her energies on trying to prove the death of her son was a homicide when in fact he had died by suicide. While there were also other complications in her grief journey, I believe this single sticking point was the primary source of her inability to engage with and effectively integrate her grief.

For grief to become active mourning, the griever is faced with the need to acknowledge the reality of the death as well as the causes and circumstances surrounding it. We as humans are capable of coping with what we know, but we cannot cope with what we do not know or are hiding from ourselves. While it is normal for the griever to move back and forth between protesting and encountering the reality of the loss (see the section on Evade-Encounter on page 159), long-term, fixed denial or sublimation result in unembarked, impasse, off-trail, or encamped grief.

Because the nature of the death associated with complicated grief is often traumatic, it is no wonder that so many grievers get stuck on Mourning Need 1. In fact, I would even say that it is normal for them to need professional help fully encountering this need. Remember that their encounters with this mourning needs must often be outsized and heroic. The realities of the causes of complicated grief are commonly horrific. And so, fully acknowledging those realities often requires looking horror full in the face and coming to terms with it, which typically causes it to lose much of its power, allowing the symptoms of shock and denial to soften.

Symptoms of an inhibition of Mourning Need 1:

In my professional experience, the primary symptoms that grievers will shine the light on when they have not sufficiently engaged with Need 1 are extended shock, numbness, denial, and/or disbelief. What in the beginning served them as a normal, temporary "time-out" from a harsh reality may have become stuck or fixed. These symptoms have now persisted in ways that have stalled their necessary grief and mourning.

Sometimes grievers who are denying or repressing the full reality of the death are unconsciously trying to reverse the death or "hold on" to the person who died. If they don't engage with the reality, their hearts whisper to them, maybe it will turn out to be unreal. Active mourning is what helps change the nature of the bonds.

In addition to shock and denial, this inability or refusal to accept the reality of the death may lead to overwhelming anxiety, clinical depression, self-punishment, and/or generalized anger at the world. Another symptom I see with an inhibition of Need 1 is pronounced or prolonged disorganization and confusion. Muddled cognition is often symptomatic of a mind and heart that have not completely come to terms with the new reality.

On the other hand, sometimes grievers who are fearful or anxious need help feeling safe in their daily lives before they are be able to set off on a genuine encounter with Need 1. This is common in traumatic grief, and processing the traumatic reality of the event of the death is often necessary before the reality of the death itself can be approached and engaged.

Alternately, practical considerations may also be a source of anxiety. A stable and secure living situation and place, adequate financial support, and help with the activities of daily living, if needed, are prerequisites to effective grief support and mourning. In fact, unstable living conditions alone can complicate grief. It's all but impossible for grievers to effectively dose themselves with the six needs of mourning if their life circumstances are such that the bottom tiers of Maslow's pyramid are not adequate and stable.

For grief companions, it is essential to recognize that when Need 1 is inhibited, all of the other mourning needs are put on hold as well. In other words, until the griever acknowledges the reality of the death, she cannot fully embrace the pain, shift the relationship from presence to memory, work to develop a new sense of identity, or search for meaning. She is also often unable to make use of support systems.

Earlier I said that though the mourning needs are numbered 1 through 6, they are not sequential. Grievers may encounter them in any order, return to random needs at any time, and work on more than one need at a time. The exception to this natural fluidity and recursiveness of grief is Need 1. Until the griever actively acknowledges the full reality of the death, the other mourning needs are largely blocked. Yes, you may witness some encountering of pain, remembering the person who died, etc., but if Need 1 is not being effectively encountered, the other needs are typically touched on shallowly and ineffectively. Because of this, I consider Need 1 a linchpin mourning need.

Facilitating active engagement with Mourning Need 1:
Following are potential helping strategies you might employ to facilitate this mourning need.

- Unembarked grief, is by definition, of course, an inhibition of Need 1. Grievers who are stuck at the trailhead of their grief wilderness need encouragement, help, and safe opportunities to tell the story of the life and the death and to talk through their challenges encountering the reality.

- If you perceive that a griever lacks understanding about the cause or circumstances of the death, it is appropriate for you to help him explore what he does and does not know about the death as well as what he may never know. After educating him about the first need of mourning and its possible role in his grief complications, you may become his advocate in obtaining additional information about the death, such as autopsy results, police reports, shared accounts of those who were present at the scene, etc.

- For carried grief, which is a form of unembarked grief, I recommend taking two steps backward with grievers to help them with a variation of Need 1, but in this case it is acknowledging the carried grief. For complicated grievers whose loss histories and family systems influences point to carried grief, it is often necessary to help them understand that their current difficulties with loss are sourced in or compounded by previous unembarked griefs. Encountering the six needs of mourning for those earlier losses is also necessary, and as grief companion, you can help them with this process. Carried grief can be like a Russian nesting doll—one grief inside another inside another— and there is no formula or lockstep procedure for getting to the center and working your way back out again. I simply suggest going slowly and letting the griever know that it is OK to work on one loss at a time.

- If the griever has been unable to tell you the story of the death— common in closed family systems—you can facilitate this process. Sharing the story aloud will help the griever move from head awareness to heart awareness of the reality of the death. In fact, there is often a need for her to tell the story many times before she is able to comprehend and fully acknowledge what has happened. Fully integrating such a painful reality is a naturally slow process. As you support this process, you are helping her internal grief become external mourning and creating divine momentum.

- A sort of back-door approach to working on this need is to help the griever explore what may be getting in the way of his acknowledgment of the reality of the death. This can be done by asking him to talk about what it is like to be in this world without the person who died. Other questions you might ask: What do you do with the love or other feelings you have that the person who died is no longer here to receive? What is a day in your life like now in contrast to what it was like before the person's death?

- Particularly when there was no funeral for the person who died (but also useful in general), consider creating a ceremony or a series of ceremonies that builds in the function of revisiting the reality of the death. I have found this to be one of the most helpful actions I can take to help complicated grievers with this need of mourning. As I often say, "When words are inadequate, have ceremony"—or, in this case, a series of ceremonies. See the purposes of ceremony shown in the pyramid graphic on page 72 to refresh your memory about the how ceremonies have unparalleled power to help grievers heal.

- You may want to encourage the griever to visit the location where the death took place. This exposure-therapy technique helps grievers who may have been avoiding the location (or cautioned by others to avoid it) to quite literally step toward the reality of the death. This activity typically helps soften denial as well as the often outsized and dirty-pain-related fear of the unknown. The visit may allow the griever to help make the unreal real and while naturally painful, it can create momentum to convert grief into mourning.

• Ask the griever to bring in photos and/or other linking objects associated with the person who died. Or better yet, make a home visit! This encourages the griever to do a life review of the person who died and helps dose him with the full reality of the death.

• With a person who likes to put words to paper, you can ❽ encourage her to write out her understanding of the death and its impact on her. At your next session, invite her to read the account aloud to you. As she speaks, you will, of course, affirm the various thoughts and feelings that come forth.

These are just a few suggested activities or techniques to facilitate the griever's active encounters with Mourning Need 1. Don't forget to look to each griever's unique strengths and ways of being as you help her with this need. For example, grievers who are naturally good helpers might be encouraged to reach out to someone else who is struggling with the same death. The encounter will likely facilitate a number of mourning needs for both grievers, including acknowledging the reality of the death.

Need 1 questions to ask yourself as you work with each unique griever:

• What is this person teaching me about what is complicating her capacity to acknowledge the reality of the death?

• What specific circumstances surrounding the death may be complicating this need?

• Are there any specific relationship issues with the person who died that make this need more complicated?

- Is there a possibility that traumatic loss has resulted in psychic numbing or acute aftershock?

- Might trauma processing be required before there can be an unfolding of the acknowledgment of the reality?

- Does this person come from a closed family system that has shut down the capacity to acknowledge loss or actively mourn?

- Do I need to respect this person's need to continue to evade or push away some of the full reality while she doses herself with the reality in bits and pieces?

- Is the griever numbing herself from facing the reality in self-destructive ways such as alcohol or drug abuse, premature involvement in new relationships, overeating, or impulsive spending?

- What can I as a companion do or be for this person to create a safe place to work on this mourning need?

Evade-Encounter ③⑦

Grievers are often surprised when I suggest to them that they must learn to befriend their grief. After all, they certainly didn't want the person they love to die, and the idea of cozying up to the death of a loved one and their painful thoughts and feelings about the loss can seem not only counterintuitive—it can seem masochistic or even crazy, especially in a culture that colludes with this misconception.

So it's important to educate grievers about the purpose of sitting with their pain and openly and honestly expressing what they are thinking and feeling (or mourning). They will find that if they learn to **encounter** their grief when it arises, both feeling it on the inside and expressing it on the outside—those painful thoughts and feelings will, over time, begin to soften. If, on the other hand, they continue to mostly deny, suppress, or distract themselves from their natural and necessary grief, the pain will not ease. What's more, it will come out in other ways, such as physical problems, mental-health challenges, relationship issues, and yes, complicated grief.

During your sessions with the complicated griever, you will be helping her do some of the hard work of encountering her grief, of course. You will also be giving her encouragement, suggestions, and support for doing more encountering in the days between sessions.

But it's also critical for you to affirm the griever's natural and necessary impulses to **evade** her grief some of the time. Grief is not just an event in time. It's not something we can wholly immerse ourselves in for a short period of time in order to "get it over with." Instead, it's something we learn to live with, that we accommodate into our continued living.

Part of that accommodation is finding a balance between grieving and living. In the early days and weeks after the death of a significant person in our lives, of course, the balance necessarily tips toward grieving. It is appropriate that our new grief is practically all-consuming, but even in those first days, we cannot do nothing but grieve. We can't, and shouldn't try to, absorb all of our grief at once. It would kill us. Instead, nature bubble-wraps us in a protective layer of shock and numbness, and we naturally turn to denial and disbelief in moments when the reality is too much to bear.

Consciously and unconsciously, we grievers also evade. We watch TV. We busy ourselves with work or chores. We go out to eat. We sleep. These forms of necessary intermittent escape make grief survivable. We also sometimes evade, however, with less healthy tactics, such as numbing ourselves with drugs or alcohol.

As time passes and we make headway in our grief journeys toward reconciliation, we begin to integrate more rewarding forms of evasion. We take vacations. We set goals and work to achieve them. We enjoy time with family and friends. Except by this point, such activities are no longer evasion—they're appropriate and meaningful life-living. The balance has shifted from primarily grief to primarily life, and eventually, if we've done the hard and ongoing work of mourning, we will have fully integrated our grief into our continued lives.

My point here is that complicated grievers also need to encounter then evade their grief. They can't work their grief 24/7 until they're healed. They too need to escape into mindless daily activities they enjoy and also work toward meaningful long-term life-living at the same time. They need you to help them find a balance between evading and encountering—a balance that's right for them at this point in their journeys. Many of them have been evading too much, by unembarking or through off-trail activities such as overworking or addictive behaviors, while others have encamped in their grief and are evading too little.

As with all things grief, there is no set evade-encounter formula. I can't give you a chart that says, "By month nine, grievers should be spending ten percent of their time in encountering their grief and 90 percent of their time evading and otherwise living." In general, though, I would suggest that complicated grievers usually need to devote more time to encountering, and they need more support in that encountering as well. But they also need affirmation that each and every day, evasion, too, is healthy and necessary if they are doing the arduous encounter work they need to do.

Evade, encounter. Encounter, evade. In grief, it's a back-and-forth seesaw that not only helps us survive but ultimately helps us learn to live our new lives and reconstruct meaning. Thank you for helping the complicated grievers in your care find the balance that will help them achieve divine momentum in their journey through their wilderness.

MOURNING NEED 2: EMBRACE THE PAIN OF THE LOSS

To be bereaved literally means "to be torn apart." When people are torn apart by complicated grief, mourning requires embracing the pain of the loss. Grievers must allow themselves to think and feel all the thoughts and feelings the death conjures as well as express those thoughts and feelings outside themselves.

This may seem backwards to you. As a mental-health caregiver, you were probably taught to treat away pain. Our culture in general has a fix-it mentality. Yet significant life losses are not really fixable, and neither is the pain that follows. Supporting a fellow human in grief is to share in her hurt, pain, fear, protest, and sadness, while recognizing I cannot take any of those feelings away.

When you as a caregiver attempt to help the griever befriend pain, you are asking her to go against her instinct to avoid pain. Complications of this need are often rooted in grievers' desire to avoid, deny, or self-treat the pain. As a consequence, it is vital to recognize grievers' natural desire to avoid or deny the pain that comes with the experience. With an awareness of timing and pacing, your role is to provide the hope and belief that while the pain hurts beyond words, she can and will have the courage to encounter it in ways that ultimately result in less pain—an amazing truth I have witnessed thousands of times.

We as humans cannot integrate loss without realizing we can survive it and imbue it with meaning. As you help the griever befriend pain, it is the hope for healing that facilitates movement out of darkness and into light.

Symptoms of pain and suffering are usually felt in five areas— physical, cognitive, emotional, social, and spiritual:

Physical: Grief naturally results in physical discomfort; the body responds to the stress of the encounter.

Cognitive: Grief naturally results in cognitive discomfort; thought processes are confused and memory is impaired.

Emotional: Grief naturally results in emotional discomfort, and a multitude of wave-like emotions (which we reviewed in Part Two) may be experienced that demand comfort and care. Note that pain isn't simply sadness; all of the emotions we covered in Part Two can be painful for the griever to experience.

Social: Grief naturally results in social discomfort; the griever may withdraw, and/or, as is common in complicated or stigmatized death circumstances, friends and family may withdraw, resulting in isolation.

Spiritual: Grief naturally results in spiritual discomfort; questions may arise such as, "Why go on living?"; "Will my life have meaning?"; "Where is God in this?"

This is always a difficult mourning need, but in complicated grief, it's common for grievers to describe the pain as much worse than the pain they experienced following other losses in life. I do not believe it is helpful to globally rank loss experiences on a pain scale (e.g., which is harder—the death of a child or the death of a soulmate?), but within an individual griever's life, she is the expert on the pain of her losses. When she says this is more painful than that or this hurts in a certain way or beyond description, she is always right.

When grievers discover that they cannot go around the pain of the loss, they often discover the courage to relax into the pain, and therein lies the paradox. Trying to avoid, repress, or deny the pain of grief makes the griever an opponent of the journey and creates more chronic states of anxiety and depression.

What's more, many friends and family members (and sometimes even caregivers) want grieving people to stay in control as a form of self-protection. Many of us attempt to control because we are afraid of the pain of grief. It hurts to embrace the depths of loss. It hurts to acknowledge that life is often dangerous, mean, and capricious and to be humbled by our life losses. Of course, as a caregiver to people in grief, you must become acquainted not only with the pain of others, but also with your own pain. If you don't, you will unconsciously want to "fix" people in pain and not create hospitality for them to dose themselves with this need.

Yes, an essential part of your helping role is to help the complicated griever dose the pain of the loss. Dosing is essential because grievers cannot (nor should they try to) overload themselves with the hurt all at one time. In fact, sometimes your role might be to distract the griever from the pain of the loss (particularly with encamped grievers), while at other times you will need to invite the griever to move toward the pain. It's an artful balance.

The fear of breaking down

In therapy, complicated grievers who are encountering Mourning Need 2 during your sessions are often afraid of losing control, breaking down, or being overwhelmed by the pain of their grief.

First, you can assure them that the sacred space that the two of you have created will accommodate whatever happens.

Second, you can affirm the normalcy of strong feelings. You have born witness to profound pain many times. It is normal, and it is necessary. You will help her dose the experience, and you will ensure that the pace and amount of expression in any one session feels safe.

And third, you can help grievers feel safer if you reframe "loss of control" as "emotional release" from the pain of loss. Help them understand that it is actually unexpressed emotions that often lead to a sense of loss of control. What's more, the pain will likely increase if it is not given the attention it demands and deserves.

Be aware that some grievers will try to keep very busy and stay on the move so the pain of the loss does not have time to catch up to them. Others will over-isolate and project an inability to find or access support. In your presence, these grievers may steer the conversation to lighter topics, make jokes, intellectualize, transfer strong feelings onto others, or talk about peripheral issues. Once your relationship is strong, you may have to supportively redirect them to do the hard work of encountering Need 2.

Symptoms of an inhibition of Mourning Need 2:

In my professional experience, the primary symptoms that grievers who are experiencing an inhibition of embracing the pain of the loss will shine the light on are fear/anxiety, protest emotions, and sadness and depression.

The opposite of embracing pain can often be seen in grievers' attempts to stay in control. Underlying that controlling impulse is fear that results in anxiety—the fear that the griever cannot tolerate the pain of the loss. This anxiety sometimes evolves to the point of panic attacks.

Note that many grievers are unaware of their fear of the pain and may instead project their anxiety onto other, seemingly unrelated concerns. They may tell you they are anxious about various life circumstances, or they may describe generalized anxiety. But in truth, the genuine source of complicated grievers' anxiety is often unengaged pain over the loss.

Protest emotions are another constellation of symptoms I have often observed in grievers who are inhibiting the pain of loss. Feelings such as anger, hate, blame, terror, resentment, rage, and jealousy commonly serve as defense mechanisms against hurt and vulnerability. What's more, explosive emotions tend to push potentially supportive family members and friends away, which keeps grievers safe from the vulnerable pain of opening up to others but also, of course, gets in the way of Need 6.

Finally and counterintuitively, grievers who are depressed are often unaware that their depression is tied to a lack of engagement with the pain of the loss in particular. Just because a griever presents as deeply sad or depressed does not mean that she is authentically encountering her grief pain. She may describe feeling sad and/or "empty," but she may not understand the need to fully embrace and express her pain over the death. Instead, she may be mired in a generalized depression, which would be eased by more focused, therapeutic encounters with her sadness, hurt, and other feelings about the death.

Facilitating active engagement with Mourning Need 2: Following are potential helping strategies you might employ to facilitate this mourning need.

- Normalize and foster the courage and momentum to experience the pain of suffering that the loss naturally invites. Help the griever understand that trying to avoid, repress, or deny the pain makes her an opponent to the journey and hinders her capacity to integrate the loss. Help her have the courage to embrace a paradox—to live in a state of both encounter and surrender while simultaneously working at and surrendering to the journey.

- Reframe the pain. Many grievers have taught me that they perceive experiencing pain as not moving forward in their grief. You can help them understand that befriending pain is actually what helps soften the pain. In other words, the pain is functional. It is naturally present for a reason. It is not only normal, it is necessary.

- Educate about and support the need to dose the pain. Some grievers will teach you that they fear moving toward the pain of loss because they believe that once they do, they won't be able to stop or will suffer a breakdown. Help them understand that they are not alone and that they will be able to tolerate the pain. You are there to be sure they are safe and to help them discover their own innate skills and strength. You are there to help them dose the pain appropriately.

- Encourage the exploration of the full gamut of thoughts and emotions. Complicated grievers will sometimes indicate that they struggle to allow themselves to experience certain thoughts or emotions. For example, a griever may teach you that in his family of origin, anger was not permitted. Now, at a time when he may need to appropriately acknowledge and express legitimate protest emotions, he is having trouble doing so. Your role is to help him feel safe enough to rewrite the "rules" he learned from a tender age. This means helping him recognize, befriend, and integrate *all* of his inner thoughts and feelings. He will see that as he befriends and expresses each thought and feeling, his anxiety about those thoughts and feelings also diminishes. It is also very helpful for the griever to realize he can experience and express intense thoughts and emotions and still survive.

- Encourage exploration backward before forward. When you observe challenges in accessing or expressing feelings related to the loss, you can invite the griever to review the circumstances of the death and tell the story of her relationship with the person who died. Those two areas of exploration often allow cathartic emotions to come to the surface, resulting in a softening of symptoms.

- The role of the therapist is to have empathy for the circumstances and adjusting the timing and pacing of helping the griever befriend the pain of the loss. Instead of trying get rid of symptoms, I'm asking myself all the time, "Where is this person teaching me he needs to go? Is it backward to the history of the relationship? Is it backward to the circumstances of the death?" Grievers whose pain is inhibited often teach me that they need more time to honor the person who died and do more memory work related to Need 3. This homeopathic approach seems to work to unfold the softening of the symptoms.

- Encourage nonverbal means of expression. Obviously, feelings are often contained in the body as well as the head and heart.

Physical activities such as painting, drawing, and exercising often facilitate the release of denied or repressed feelings. Listening to evocative music, planting a memorial garden, sewing a quilt, participating in memory walks—any activity that marries memory work with physical activity may help grievers even more than verbal expression alone. As you learn about the specific interests, gifts, and skills of each griever, you will be looking for tailored opportunities.

• Consider the use of ceremony to provide the structure to engage with and integrate challenging thoughts and emotions as well as invite recall, allow for a search for meaning, and create additional support systems. For some powerful feelings, words alone are inadequate. Surrounding them with ceremony is what we as humans have done since time immemorial. You will find that well-planned and well-executed ceremonies help complicated grievers feel safer in encountering the raw emotions that most overwhelm them.

• Be aware that some grievers don't think of their suffering as something they want to reconcile. Encamped grievers, in particular, may, consciously or unconsciously, perceive their pain as the only way to stay connected to the person who died. Sadly, these grievers run the risk of dying while they are alive. When this is what the person teaches you, your role becomes one of trying to help her find appropriate ways to still have a connection to the person who died while finding meaning in continued living. (See Mourning Needs 3 and 5 for more thoughts on how to do this.)

These are just a few suggested activities or techniques to facilitate the griever's active encounters with Mourning Need 2. I encourage you to look for clues the griever is giving you and match techniques to her unique symptoms.

Need 2 questions to ask yourself as you work with each unique griever:

- What is this person teaching me about what is complicating her capacity to embrace the pain of the loss?

- What specific circumstances around the death or the history of the relationship interface with complicating this need?

- What symptoms is this person presenting with that reflect potential inhibition of this need?

- Has the griever ever had the pain that accompanies grief normalized? How or how not?

- Are there any potential fears of what will happen if she allows herself to surrender to the pain of the loss?

- Does the griever come from a closed family system that inhibited the capacity to befriend the pain of loss?

- What can I do to create a safe place for the griever to work on this need?

Educating complicated grievers as part of the care plan

Understandably, complicated grievers are often confused about what they're experiencing. After all, it's out of the ordinary. What's more, our grief-avoidant culture and common grief misconceptions may also be contributing to their befuddlement. So as we've said, part of your role is to educate grievers along the way. What information you choose to share depends on the needs of the unique mourner. Among the topics you might interweave into your sessions are the following. Handouts that cover these topics are included in the

Complicated Grief Educational Supplement, available at www.centerforloss.com.

- *The griever's unique complicating factors.* **6** Grievers deserve to understand why their grief is complicated. They also benefit from going over the care plan you create to assist them, including its expected duration.

- *The value of "dosing" the pain of the loss.* **37** In other words, conveying the value of evade-encounter as normal to integrating loss. Of interest is that this need to slow down and respect grievers' defenses allows them to feel safe enough to befriend the pain.

- *The need for good self-care in grief.* **39** Grievers should be encouraged to get enough rest and hydration, take a 20 to 30 minute walk each day, seek and accept social support, and make use of activities that allow for the conversion of grief into mourning.

- *The importance of not self-treating the pain.* **21** Grievers who self-treat with alcohol, drugs, or other means often get stuck in off-trail grief, further complicating their journeys.

- *The concept of active work on the six needs of mourning.* **29** This is a definable, manageable concept that grievers understand and feel empowered by.

- *The normalcy of the symptoms of grief.* **14** Grievers need to know the symptoms of grief, including those that some may think are inappropriate, such as griefbursts.

- *Common misconceptions about grief and mourning.* **10** It's typical for some of these to be fueling the complications of the grief experience.

- *The normalcy of continued love for the person who died.* **16**
  Many grievers are relieved to be educated early in the
  counseling relationship that they don't have to "let go."
  Others—the encamped grievers—are afraid that allowing
  their pain to soften will mean breaking all ties to the person
  who died.

MOURNING NEED 3: REMEMBER THE PERSON WHO DIED
After the death of someone loved, grievers have a need to pursue
a relationship of memory with the person who died. It is also
appropriate and meaningful for the billions of grievers who believe
that life continues after death to shift the relationship from one of
presence on Earth to one of presence separated, for the time being,
by time and space. Either way, the love and attachment remain, but
the focus of that love and attachment shift from one of presence to
one of (at least for the time being) memory.

Another way to think of this mourning need comes to us from
storytelling. Human beings are wired for narrative. Our minds and
hearts make sense of things through story. First this happened,
then this happened, and because of that, this happened next…
When we tell ourselves and others our most important stories, we
begin to make sense of them. We naturally shape the events, which
might seem fragmented or dissonant on the surface, into a cohesive
and coherent whole. And while the constructed story is helpful
to grievers, it is the process of storytelling—often over and over,
as many times as is necessary—that provides divine momentum.
Storying is so powerful that its place in the companion's toolkit
cannot be overestimated.

In cases of complicated grief, however, the need to remember is
often—you can probably guess what I'm going to say next—extra

complicated. If the griever's relationship with the person who died was unhealthy, for example, the griever will naturally struggle with challenging memories. Alternately, some grievers in this situation prefer not to remember too clearly or thoroughly because they are invested in a handful of memories that portray an inaccurately rosy or one-dimensional picture of the relationship. Being asked to remember too much may painfully poke holes in the façade. What's more, if the griever has been contaminated by societal or family systems misconceptions that "the past is in the past" and she needs to "carry on," she may resist remembering, thinking it counterproductive or saying, "Why remember? It won't bring him back." And of course, when circumstances of the death were traumatic, memories of the death event itself may necessarily threaten to take over the memory spotlight for a long period of time. These and other complicated grief risk factors often combine to make remembering the person who died a more challenging process.

Yet despite the surfeit of challenges in complicated grief, remembering is essential. In grief, it is necessary to go backward before going forward, and storying is often a vital part of how moving backward creates the momentum to eventually go forward. What I have learned in my professional experience is that circumventing memories invites unembarked grief. It's like leaving a significant portion of a wound uncleansed and uncared for, on purpose. While all grief care must be individualized, and the unique needs and circumstances of any particular griever must take precedence over generalizations, creating safe conditions for and encouraging the appropriate sharing of difficult memories is an essential part of the search-and-rescue work of companioning complicated grievers. Inviting grievers to retell the story to reconcile the loss and acknowledge/express feelings is an essential helping role of the therapist. As a matter of fact, counselors who lack an understanding or are uncomfortable with this retelling and revisiting process would probably be better served to consider another line of work.

Yes, I strongly believe that to ignore painful or ambivalent memories is to prevent healing from taking place. In the safety of your nonjudgmental relationship, and with the right timing and pacing, you must invite complicated grievers to share their memories with you. Memories and grief must have a heart to hold them. In fact, remembering the past is what makes hoping for the future possible.

However, it's also important to note that in some complicated grievers—usually encamped grievers—an unflagging impulse to retell the story can reflect a defense against integration of the six needs of mourning and a desire to come to reconcile the loss. There is a difference between processing emotions in ways that integrate them versus retelling but not experiencing any change and movement. This integration requires grievers to identify, feel, explore, give some aspect of expression to, and work through whatever feelings fit with their experience.

In complicated grief the defenses are, in fact, the areas that need to be given attention. The defense of retelling with a lack of desire for movement must be related to with sensitivity and compassion. In my experience, this form of retelling must gradually interface with Mourning Need 5. Active, engaged mourning around the search for meaning is what often softens the retelling process over time. In other words, if there is a lack of meaning, there is a lack of movement.

Symptoms of an inhibition of Mourning Need 3:
In my professional experience, the primary symptoms that the griever will shine the light on that indicate an inhibition of this

mourning need are disorientation, confusion, explosive emotions, guilt, and sadness and depression. Any of these symptoms can invite me to explore with grievers where they are in this process of remembering and shifting the relationship from one of presence to one of memory.

Disorientation and confusion—which may come across as scatteredness, an incapacity to focus, or an inability to accomplish the essential tasks of daily living—may indicate an inhibition of the need to engage with memories of the person who died because when grievers push aside memories, they are often unable to focus sufficiently on anything else. Consciously or unconsciously, they're often suppressing memory work (fearing the reality and the pain), and the result is that they're distracted by the effort and mind tricks it takes to them to suppress. They may be able to keep a deep engagement with memories at bay, but in doing so they're using up a lot of their RAM on avoidance and distraction.

Explosive emotions may also be symptomatic of an inhibition of this mourning need. If my child dies by suicide, for example, I will naturally be challenged by the need to recall the event of the death as well as earlier memories, good and bad. It's just too painful to remember. Anger feels better. It creates a kind of filter that transforms pain into rage. As with Needs 1 and 2, however, authentic encounters with Need 3 will almost always soften protest emotions.

Of course, the care-eliciting symptoms of guilt, regret, and self-reproach may be tied to an insufficient encounter with Need 3 as well. Feelings of guilt tend to stem from one or a handful of memories. It's human nature to focus on the certain moments in a relationship that we wish would have gone differently. Hindsight, as they say, is 20-20, and we all carry with us those "If only I'd ..." or "I just feel so bad that..." regrets. But converting her relationship with the person who died from one of presence to one of memory requires the griever to broadly encounter memories from the full sweep of the relationship. Exploring memories of all kinds and from all points on the timeline of the relationship—happy, silly, angry, sad, boring; significant, average, trivial; early, middle, late—will help the griever put any regrettable moments into context. Just as a person's life cannot be defined by a single moment, neither can a relationship. It is not your job to overtly teach the griever this lesson, but in encouraging her to recall the full gamut of memories, you will be helping her come to this important realization herself.

Finally, grievers experiencing complicated grief with pronounced sadness or depression often need dosing with Need 3 as well. Grievers who suffered a traumatic loss, for example, may be understandably stuck on perseverating about the event of the death and may need encouragement to slowly and gently embrace memories of the relationship. Other complicated grievers may be ruminating about memories without expressing them. Actively engaging with memories through telling stories, reviewing photos, making memory albums, and other activities often transforms despair into hope. Yes, active remembering is often difficult and painful, both for the griever and for the therapist, but creating an environment in which pain is welcomed is an essential part of your role. In my experience, grievers who are invited to spend time sharing memories will often end up smiling through their tears. Their sadness and depression, which had hardened, now begin to soften through active and ongoing memory work.

Facilitating active engagement with Mourning Need 3:
Following are potential helping strategies you might employ to facilitate this mourning need.

- Seek an understanding of the inhibition to work on this need. This discovery process will provide the direction of how you can explore any fear about this backward work, address it, and help the griever discover the courage to do the work.

- Assist the griever in understanding that is in going backward and reviewing the relationship that she will ultimately be able to start moving forward again. Until she understands and believes this, she is at risk for trying to push herself forward in the absence of the backward work that is necessary.

- Ask the griever to bring in photos and/or other linking objects associated with the person who died. Invite her to refer to the photos and objects in telling you stories about the person who died and the relationship they shared.

- Legitimizing memory work is just that—work. Some people will teach you that they perceive no value in going backward. This is not uncommon in our culture, which often projects the need to keep "moving forward" and "putting the past in the past."

- While bringing sensitivity to timing and pacing, encourage a comprehensive review of the relationship, from the time the griever and the loved one met to the time of the death. Ask the griever to describe the nature of the connection as well as good times in the relationship, bad times in the relationship, specific challenges, mutual interests and values, dissimilar interests and values, etc.

- Explore the various emotions that evolve from the relationship review. This often allows a softening of the emotional bond of the attachment. This does not mean that the griever is "letting go" but instead appropriately shifting the nature of the relationship.

- Provide space to give attention to unpleasant memories. Obviously, this reality makes integrating this need more naturally complicated. Yet, to ignore painful or ambivalent memories is to prevent healing from taking place. In the safety of your nonjudgmental, empathetic relationship and with the right timing and pacing, the griever can explore these memories with you.

- Help the person acknowledge any sense of "unfinished business" that may exist concerning his relationship with the person who died. This demands mourning because it reflects an emotional form of attachment. It is your role as a companion to help her give this unfinished business the attention it demands.

- Gently remind the griever that memories and grief must have a heart to hold them. Remind her that going to the past makes hoping for the future possible. Remind her that the essence of finding meaning in the future is not to forget the past but to embrace and integrate it into her life's story.

Need 3 questions to ask yourself as you work with each unique griever:

- What is the person teaching me about what is complicating his capacity to shift the relationship from presence to memory?

- What specific circumstances surrounding the death may be complicating this need? Sudden, traumatic death naturally creates more evasion, which slows this process down.

- Are there any specific relationship issues that make this need more complicated?

- Has the person been told to "move forward" or "let go" in ways that inhibit this need?

- Does the griever fear that backward-looking memory work will reveal things that she prefers not to look at?

- Is the griever resisting the shift in the relationship in an effort to deny the reality of the death?

- What can I as a companion do or be for this person to create a safe place to work on this need?

WHEN GRIEF IS COMPLICATED

Working with traumatized grievers

As I mentioned in Part One, many traumatized grievers present with psychic numbing or acute aftershock. They are often initially (and understandably) focused on the details of the event of the death. They may teach you they are reliving the event and have intrusive thoughts about what happened. They may express that their bodies hurt, with symptoms reflecting the experience of being torn apart. Their ability to function day-to-day is often severely compromised, and it's common for them to find it impossible to focus on work or whatever their everyday responsibilities are. It's also common for them to feel drawn to Need 5, as the search for meaning compels them to ask lots of "why" questions. They may also experience feelings of hopelessness, protest, and anxiety. Sometimes they do not even relate their hyper-vigilance and anxiety to the event of the death.

Traumatized grievers need additional safety and trust in the holding environment you work to create. Trauma experiences are influenced by a more primary system of the brain than grief. This system (which initiates fight, flight, or freeze) calls upon grievers to feeling safe and secure first, and then and only then, slowly approaching the raw grief to convert it to active mourning.

Because they typically feel violated, unsafe, and out of control, I like to give traumatized grievers control over deciding when and how to explore details surrounding the death. Allow them to set the pace; you will need to go slowly. If you push instead of follow, traumatized grievers will often feel further violated, and you run the risk of increasing their anxiety (to the point of dissociation, total shut-down, or panic attack) as well as damaging their trust in you. You must meet traumatized grievers where they are before any movement can take place.

Your compassionate presence will allow traumatized grievers to dose the experience, as they are able and willing. As one homicide survivor taught me, "I had to fill in all of the data from the trauma—What happened to my child?—before I could mourn the loss of her." Understanding and respecting this necessary sequencing demands emotional intelligence on the part of the therapist as well as patience. The 11 tenets of companioning will remind you to go slow and take the back seat. There are no rewards for speed!

While I have found that building trust in the relationship, establishing safety, and going very slowly —combined with solid therapeutic skills—are enough to eventually help the griever move beyond fear-based traumatic grief responses and on to the work of mourning, trauma processing techniques such as cognitive behavioral therapy, hypnotherapy, and EMDR may be used to process the trauma before grief companioning gets underway. If you need help working with traumatized grievers, reach out for professional mentorship and referral options in your community.

MOURNING NEED 4: DEVELOP A NEW SELF-IDENTITY
This need of mourning relates to the necessary evolution of a new self-identity based on life as it is now, after the death of the loved one, versus life as it was then, before the death. All of us are forever changed by significant loss. After the deaths of my elderly parents, for example, I had to struggle through a period of acknowledging

and embracing the odd and painful reality that I was now an adult orphan. Over time, my sense of self necessarily changed, and the dynamics within my family necessarily changed.

Such self-transformation is never easy, but it's especially challenging in cases of complicated grief. When the relationship torn apart by death was particularly close, complicated grievers tend to struggle a great deal with this mourning need. Often, a big part of their sense of self, not to mention their daily schedules, revolved around the person who died. Soulmates, life partners, parents and children, siblings, work partners, and others typically fall into this category. Add in another risk factor or two (or more) from Part One of this book and it's understandable why reconstructing self-identity is often so painful and arduous for these grievers.

It is not uncommon for grievers to feel angry, helpless, frustrated, inadequate, and/or afraid as they work on this mourning need. Uncomfortable feelings of heightened dependence on others are also typical, as are struggles with self-worth.

Redefinition of the self in the aftermath of a complicated loss is usually a long, slow process. I will also add that as they work on this need, many grievers ultimately discover some positive aspects of their changed selves. They may be surprised to meet a new confidence in themselves, for example. They may uncover a more caring, kind, and sensitive part of themselves. They may develop an assertive part of their identities that empowers them to go on living fully even though they continue to feel a deep sense of loss.

People can and do change for the better. People grow, and devastating grief can be the catalyst. It is growth that requires a deep sacrifice, however—a sacrifice no one would choose if undoing it were possible. I know that, and you know that. But because undoing death is not possible, growth through grief is the best possible outcome. As you companion complicated grievers, part of your role is to notice and affirm such "growth spurts" as they occur. Fostering hope and meaning in grievers' continuing lives means celebrating their mourning progress as well as their growth.

Symptoms of an inhibition of Mourning Need 4:

In my professional experience, the primary symptoms that grievers will express related to an inhibition of this mourning need are extended shock, searching and yearning, anxiety, explosive emotions, guilt and regret, and sadness and depression. As we've discussed, these symptoms may also be related to other mourning needs as well, but especially in cases of an exceptionally close or difficult relationship with the person who died, I always invite grievers to explore where they are in the process of reconstructing their self-identities.

Extended shock is common among grievers who had a close day-to-day relationship with the person who died, in part because their own existence is so very different now. Not only is someone they loved dearly no longer physically present to them, but often their mornings are different. Their afternoons are different. Their evenings are different. The places they go, the activities they do, the conversations they have, the tasks they accomplish—all may be completely changed. It's no wonder that for these grievers, that stunned state of shock and disbelief may go on for quite some time. Devoting time and energy to an ongoing exploration and recreation of self-identity will naturally soften these symptoms.

Searching and yearning are also normal, but in hyper-dependent relationships, they typically become even more pronounced. Grievers often describe expecting the person who died to walk through the door, just as he always had, but people with an inhibition of Need 4 may go even further, describing actively visiting certain places to look for the person who died or continuing to spend an inordinate amount of time at the final resting place. Yearning is typically described as, "I can't stop thinking about her" or "All I want to do is be with her again." Again, reconstructing self-identity will naturally take a long time, but a little work on this need each week will give the griever divine momentum, and these symptoms will ease.

Change makes most of us security-craving, routine-loving humans feel ill at ease, and not knowing who we are all of a sudden is an extreme instance of this. So we feel anxious. People in complicated grief may feel especially anxious, as their complex relationship and life ties to the person who died (not to mention potential preexisting personality issues and more) often affect their self-identities on many levels.

When guilt and regret are pronounced or prolonged, compassionate and timely dosing with various of the six needs of mourning may be called for, especially Need 4. This is because developing a new self-identity includes coming to terms with the limits of one's former self-identity and self-responsibility. Exploring issues of self-identity helps grievers reconstruct the boundaries and strengths of self.

Anger and other explosive emotions may also arise with an inhibition of Need 4 because people generally do not like having their self-identities ripped away from them. They are often, understandably, mad. A parent of a child who died, for example, may be angry for many reasons, but one of those reasons is likely the fracturing of the sense of self he had established as a father. That identity was attacked and perhaps shattered. He may be angry at both the loss of his old earned self-identity and the fact that he is being forced to create a new one.

Last but never least, sadness and depression may be symptomatic of a lack of an ongoing or effective encounter with Need 4. Like

Need 5, the search for meaning, which we'll discuss next, Need 4 is in large part forward-looking (though the need for backward-looking self-identity review comes first). Grievers whose self-identities were wholly or mostly intertwined with a life spent with the person who died will often feel nothingness or despair looking forward. After all, they are now ciphers (not actually, but in their self-understanding), so how can they possibly become whole people again in the future? As one complicated griever whose wife died told me, "I have taken training courses, traveled, volunteered, given myself peaceful time, etc. However, the reality is that nothing has helped. I still come home to an empty house with no one to share my life with." While her situation was multifaceted, clearly this griever had not yet begun to shift her self-identity to that of someone who is capable and deserving of establishing new partner relationships.

Facilitating active engagement with Mourning Need 4:
Following are potential helping strategies you might employ to facilitate this mourning need.

- Seek an understanding of the inhibition to work on this need. For example, was there hyper-dependence in the relationship to the exclusion of support systems? This discovery process will give you direction about what the griever needs to give attention to.

- Explore whether or not people in the griever's support circle have supported his need to mourn the lost sense of identity. Loss of sense of self is a common major secondary loss that needs to be legitimized and normalized, both by you and by others. If that has not happened, part of your helping role is to listen, bear witness, and empathize with this aspect of the loss. It is also appropriate for the griever to invite one or two main support people to a counseling session for discussion and education about this mourning need.

- Has anyone around the griever over-functioned for her? For example, an adult child who totally takes over and does everything for a surviving parent may in effect be inhibiting this necessary mourning need. By contrast, has anyone around the griever under-functioned for her? For example, friends or family members who project that a 75-year-old who has never balanced a checkbook should be able to instantly do so are likely denying the griever's need to mourn the old self-identity before reconstructing a new one. Again, education and empathy are key tools.

- Was the griever's self-esteem dependent on the appraisal of the person who died? Did challenges in the griever's childhood impact self-esteem? Normalizing blows to self-esteem is an essential part of companioning. In addition, when the timing is right, recommending outside activities that build self-esteem will often help the griever work on Mourning Need 4 as well as several others at the same time. Activities he enjoys typically fall into this category. Spending time with people who provide nurturance and support also boosts self-esteem. Finally, invite him to eventually help others in need, as this engages the griever in the world around him.

- A grief diary, or journal, can be a powerful tool to assist people with complicated grief. Inviting the griever to write about her grief for a few minutes at the beginning or end of each day may help her with not only Need 4 but all the others as well. The error I see some grief counselors make, however, is prescribing journaling to each and every person they see. Not everyone is a journaler. If you tell me you have never so much as written a postcard and I tell you to journal your grief, it will likely not work. A treater would prescribe a journal to every griever; a companion would allow each griever to teach if journaling is a good fit. For grievers who might benefit from journaling, you may want to consider providing griever-led writing prompts each week, on loss issues and mourning needs that suit the griever's current grief work. Some counselors and support groups use my *Understanding Your Grief* book in combination with its accompanying journal, *The Understanding Your Grief Journal*.

Need 4 questions to ask yourself as you work with each unique griever:

- What is this person teaching me about what is complicating her capacity to develop a new self-identity?

- What specific circumstances surrounding the death (such as suicide, unexpected death, or long-term caregiver role) may be complicating this need?

- Are there any specific relationship issues that make this need more complicated, such as hyper-dependence, ambivalence, or a history of abuse? What was the strength of the attachment? Was this a soulmate relationship? Was this an abusive relationship?

- Are there naturally difficult practical role changes that are challenging this griever? This often comes into play for grievers whose new need to be self-sufficient is made more difficult because they have never shopped for groceries, filled a gas tank, mowed the lawn, driven a car, balanced a checkbook, etc.

- What is the griever's attitude about learning new roles or tasks that were previously filled by the person who died? What is the griever's general ability or desire to adapt to change?

- What can I as a companion do or be for this person to create a safe place to work on this need?

Ritual of reception

Over the years I have discovered the value of a simple spiritual practice I use to prepare my heart and soul to be present to grievers with humility, unknowing, and unconditional love. I have come to refer to this practice as my "readiness to receive" ritual.

Just before I see anyone for support in their journey, I center myself in a quiet place, inside or outside the Center for Loss and Life Transition. By creating a sacred space and stepping away from the demands of the day, I seek to find quiet and stillness. In a very real sense, I'm preparing my soul to be totally present to the grieving person or family. This practice is a way of letting go of anything that might get in the way of my open-heartedness. I seem to need this time to listen to myself before I can listen to others.

Once I have gone quiet, I repeat a three-phrase mantra to myself:

"No rewards for speed."

"Not attached to outcome."

"Divine momentum."

These words help me slow down, recognize my role is to help create momentum for the griever to authentically mourn, and remember the vital importance of being present to people where they are instead of where I might think they need to be. After repeating these phrases for two to three minutes— almost in meditation—I usually conclude with some sort of affirmation like, "I thank the universe for providing me the opportunity to help people mourn well so they can go on to live well and love well."

I encourage you to try my ritual of reception or create your own. Anything that helps prepare you to be present to grievers and embody the companioning philosophy will work.

MOURNING NEED 5: SEARCH FOR MEANING

This need relates to renewing one's rationale for life and living after it has been torn apart. After a significant loss, grievers naturally question the meaning and purpose of life. They also work to shape compelling reasons to go on. They review their philosophy of life and explore religious and spiritual values as they work on this need.

I would say that most if not all of the risk factors for complicated grief we reviewed in Part One of this primer may be ingredients in the pronounced search for meaning typical of complicated grief. That's because none of it makes sense to the griever. The manner of death, the untimeliness of the death, the lack of support, the concurrent stressors, the mismatch with preexisting faith—these and other complicators often naturally engender a confusing and laborious search for meaning. Why is this happening? Why in this way? Why is everything so hard for me in particular?

Note that "Why" questions often precede "How" questions when it comes to the search for meaning. Grievers need to puzzle through *why* things matter anymore before they can begin to reconstruct the practical path of *how* they will proceed in life. This search for reasons to go on living is a vital part of grief work and requires a heroic expenditure of physical, cognitive, emotional, social, and spiritual energy.

Complicated loss forces grievers to explore their worldviews— that set of beliefs they have about how the universe functions and what place they, as individuals, occupy therein. Some studies have observed that many people in modern Western culture tend to travel through life believing that the world is essentially a nice place to live, that life is mostly fair, and that they are basically good people who deserve to have good things happen to them. But when a traumatic loss event happens, the pain and suffering undermine these beliefs and can make it very difficult to continue living this illusorily happy life. The result is that through the search for meaning, pain and suffering are often intensified, at least in the beginning.

So where do complicated grievers begin their search for meaning and renewal of resources for life and living? For many, the search begins with their religious or spiritual traditions. Doubt often arises. For example, in the Judeo-Christian tradition, a foundational belief is that the universe was created by a good and just God. Complicated loss naturally challenges many grievers' belief in the goodness of God as well as their understanding that the world is essentially a nice place in which to live.

When such beliefs or longstanding worldviews are challenged in early grief, there is often little, if anything, to replace them right away. This is part of the "suspension" or "void" that grief initiates—an absence of belief that precedes any renewal of belief. This absence creates liminal space. *Limina* is the Latin word for "threshold," the space betwixt and between. When grievers are in liminal space, they are not busily and unthinkingly going about their daily lives. Neither are they living from a place of assuredness about their relationships and beliefs. Instead, they are unsettled. Both their mindless daily routines and their core beliefs have been shaken, forcing them to reconsider who they are, why they're here, and what life means. It's frightening and unpleasant being in liminal space, but that's where complicated grief takes them. Without loss (which they didn't ask for, by the way), they wouldn't go there. But here's the thing: It is only in liminal space that they can reconstruct their shattered worldviews and re-emerge as transformed, whole people who are ready to live fully again.

Bringing one's torn-apart world back together takes time, loving companions, and humility—that virtue that helps us humans when we are forced to admit powerlessness. A vital part of helping complicated grievers search for meaning is bearing witness to their natural struggles without trying to fill the void with easy answers or quick fixes. They have profound meaning-of-life questions for which they—not you—must find answers.

Creating sacred space where grievers can hurt and eventually find meaning in continued living are not mutually exclusive. Actually, the need to openly mourn and the need to slowly discover renewed meaning in continued living can and do naturally blend into each other, with the former giving way to the latter as healing unfolds.

Symptoms of an inhibition of Mourning Need 5:
In my professional experience, the primary symptoms that grievers will express related to an inhibition of this mourning need are disorganization, anxiety, explosive emotions, regret, sadness and depression, and difficulties with trust and intimacy.

Complicated grievers often feel at loose ends. They may express that they struggle with not knowing what to focus on each day, having trouble concentrating, or being ineffective at accomplishing anything. Fundamentally, these symptoms are often a struggle with meaning and purpose. After all, if you haven't recreated a sense of meaning in your life, what does it matter if you make your bed or exercise or work toward future goals? Purpose is what drives all of us, and a lack of purpose—which is a common natural consequence of devastating loss—leaves us foundering. Before grievers can reestablish the "hows" of daily living, they need to invest time and energy into exploring the "whys" of daily living.

Similarly, as grief companion, you will also see anxiety related to the search for meaning. We talked about liminal space—the place betwixt and between. When we're in liminal space, we feel anxious. It's uncomfortable. It's unsettling. We're uprooted, and we haven't yet set down new roots. That sense of being adrift in grief occasionally feels freeing to grievers—they now have a chance to start over, to forge a new path or reinvest in once-cherished activities they set aside long ago—but more often it feels stressful and frightening.

Anger and other protest emotions may indicate an inhibition of Mourning Need 5 as well. Understandably, people get mad when traumatic loss circumstances shatter their lives and their hearts. They will often talk about being angry about the unfairness, the injustice, the violence, or the untimeliness. At bottom, these are all meaning-of-life concerns. It's unfair that bad things happen to good people. It's enraging that some families experience multiple losses in one event or sequentially. Some parents, for example, suffer not only the death of a child but the deaths of more than one child. Focusing on the search for meaning is never easy in such circumstances, but over time and with a great deal of arduous work, it leads to a softening of explosive emotions and a more tenderhearted encounter with grief.

Regret and the search for meaning often go hand-in-hand as well because it requires the reconstruction of meaning for grievers to find ways to integrate feelings of guilt, regret, or unfinished business. Essentially, they have to figure out where the regrets fit, for them, in the scheme of things. Maybe they find ways to forgive themselves that fit with a new or renewed outlook on life and death. Perhaps they ultimately decide to give them over to God or to the human condition. Maybe they choose to atone for past missteps through service to others. Regardless of the path each individual griever opts to take, their search for meaning forces them to genuinely encounter their regrets and reconcile them into their continued living.

Challenges with the search for meaning, mourning Need 5, are common among grievers mired in despair. They may make it clear to you that they're struggling with finding reasons to put their feet on the floor in the morning. In this case, you can help by acting as a witness and sounding board to this struggle and, when the timing is right, by challenging the griever to build new meaning.

Of course, it's easy to understand how the search for meaning and sadness and depression fit together. When grievers are depressed, they often feel like life has no meaning. Or they are deeply sad that the meaning that used to form the very foundation of their life has now been shattered. Yes, the death of a significant person may create ripple-effect losses of many kinds, but I would argue that the loss of meaning is often the most challenging to encounter—even more challenging sometimes than the loss of the physical presence of the person who died. Judicious and ongoing dosing with Need 5 often helps complicated grievers begin to find toeholds in their search for meaning impasse.

There are often no easy answers in this search, but time spent exploring the questions and engaging with spiritual practices typically attenuates this normal and necessary symptom.

Facilitating active engagement with Mourning Need 5:
Following are potential helping strategies you might employ to facilitate this mourning need.

- As noted under Need 1, there is a critical interface between acknowledging the reality of the death and searching for continued meaning in life. If a griever in your care is struggling with Need 5, ask yourself if he has thoroughly and authentically acknowledged the reality of the death, not only with his head but with his heart. This critical sequencing issue sometimes manifests as an inability to reconstruct meaning when in truth it is more an impasse of Need 1.

- Once the griever has done a lot of storytelling and life and relationship review with you, it's appropriate for you to work on helping the griever see patterns and themes of various kinds. One of the patterns you will notice is activities and people that give the griever a sense of meaning and purpose. Affirming these activities and people can help the griever understand where to go looking and reach out for renewed meaning. You might say, for example, "I've noticed that whenever you talk about your horses, your eyes light up and your whole being gets energized. I've also noticed that you really seem to enjoy spending time with young people. Have you thought about combining the two things?"

- Spending a few minutes at the close of each session discussing "reasons to get my feet out of bed this week" may be an excellent use of time. While the search for meaning is more broadly existential, it's also very common for grievers to struggle with day-to-day motivation and meaning. You might even suggest that the griever make a quick written list to tape to the mirror over his sink.

- Because the journey through grief is most fundamentally a spiritual journey of the heart and soul, it only makes sense that you would invite the griever to explore spiritual questions during your sessions as well as spend some time each day on spiritual activities. What those activities are will depend on the griever's beliefs and predilections, but they might include prayer, meditation, yoga, spiritual readings, attendance at places of worship, and more. Remember, it's not your job to find meaning for the griever, but it is your job to encourage an authentic and ongoing encounter with the search for meaning. Ask the griever to report on spiritual matters each session, and affirm any natural spiritual questioning or anger the griever may be experiencing.

- Especially in cases of complicated grief, grievers often feel that the meaning rug has been pulled out from under them. Something so terrible has happened that any beliefs or equilibrium they may have had in the past may now be seriously damaged or even destroyed. And so, complicated grievers often need extra time and care in exploring and expressing their former sense of meaning and spiritual beliefs as well as what happened to that sense and those beliefs when the person they love died. In other words, complicated grief often requires a great deal of extra backward-looking meaning review and exploration before it's appropriate to work on the forward-looking search for meaning. As always, follow the griever's cues and remember that there are no rewards for speed. Take it slow.

- Grievers' divine sparks are made stronger by people and activities that give them a sense of meaning. Phrases people use to describe this feeling of passion and purpose are "It makes me feel alive," "I lose myself in it," and "I feel like it's what I'm meant to do." Sometimes grievers need affirmation that it's OK to drop activities and people that sap them of energy and devote more time to activities and people that give them that buzz of meaning.

- When the time is right, which will usually be a number of sessions into your time together, you might ask the griever to work on a personal mission statement and/or vision board as homework for the next session.

- Keep in mind the concept of heroic mourning. Because the griever's loss circumstances were likely epic, her mourning work must be equally epic. The passage through the wilderness will be more arduous and require greater feats of daring and perseverance. It will also take longer. Grand gestures may be called for in her search for meaning.

Need 5 questions to ask yourself as you work with each unique griever:

- What is this person teaching me about what is complicating his capacity to search for meaning?

- Which specific relationship issues or circumstances surrounding the death (such as suicide, unexpected death, or out-of-order death) may be complicating this need?

- What is the griever's religious and spiritual history? What are her belief systems and practices today? Is she spending time every day on her spirit? If not, how can I help companion her in caring for her spiritual self?

- Have I adequately encouraged and made space and time for the backward-looking search for meaning before encouraging the griever's forward-looking search for meaning?

- As I am privileged to bear witness to this unique griever's thoughts, feelings, and stories, what patterns or themes am I noticing about what has given his life meaning? How can I mine those patterns to help reveal meaningful life choices moving forward?

- What can I as a companion do or be for this person to create a safe place to work on this need?

MOURNING NEED 6: RECEIVE AND ACCEPT ONGOING SUPPORT FROM OTHERS

This need acknowledges and emphasizes that complicated grievers need support long after the event of the death. Because mourning is a dosed process that unfolds over time, support must be available for not just months but years after the death. The quality and quantity of support the griever receives is a major influence on his capacity to integrate the loss into his life and renew resources for living.

Unfortunately, because our society places so much emphasis on returning to "normal" shortly after a death, many grieving people are soon abandoned by supporters in their lives. When possible, an essential part of your companioning role is to support the griever not only through the roughest part of her journey but over the long term.

To be truly helpful, the people who make up the support system must appreciate the impact the event and its secondary losses have had and are continuing to have on the griever. They must understand that in order to slowly reconcile the losses, the griever must be allowed—even encouraged—to mourn long after the death. And they must perceive grief not as an enemy to be vanquished but as a necessity to be experienced as a result of having established meaningful bonds in life.

As you care for the complicated griever, you will learn about the support he may or may not receive from individual family members or friends, from faith communities, or from other groups that are a part of his life. Some grievers will teach you that they are essentially alone now in life, or that they feel completely alone. Because this need of mourning, like the other five, is not optional, part of your role for isolated grievers is to mentor them, slowly and over time, in finding ways to help them reach out and connect socially. For many introverted grievers, the support of just one loyal friend is enough to make all the difference. Identifying and more deeply bonding with that friend may be part of Need 6.

You will also learn that some grievers openly seek and accept support, while others are more likely to have difficulty engaging with the support that is available to them. Accepting support may be made more difficult by preexisting personality issues, family systems challenges, or a complex loss history.

Some complicated grievers will teach you that the stigmatized circumstances of the loss (such as suicide or drug overdose) have impacted the offering of support from others. Often, the greater the stigma, the less the support available and the higher the risk for mutual pretense, which is when people around the griever know what has happened but believe they should not talk about it with the griever. The griever himself may also participate in this pretense.

Obviously, the griever will need extra support on certain days or times of the year. For example, birthdays, holidays, and the anniversary of the death will often naturally trigger griefbursts—heightened periods of sadness and loss that can be assuaged by ongoing support.

A vital part of your search-and-rescue role is to be among those whom the griever knows she can depend on to understand that her grief will continue long after society deems appropriate. It is also appropriate for you to educate the griever's closest family members and friends about the six needs of mourning in general and her needs in particular.

Symptoms of an inhibition of Mourning Need 6:

In my professional experience, the primary symptoms that grievers will shine the light on related to an inhibition of this mourning need are disbelief, anxiety, sadness and depression, and difficulties with trust and intimacy.

A prolonged sense of disbelief and numbness may point in part to a challenge with Need 6 because the shared social response to loss—in part the function of the funeral but also of social mourning norms in general, including visits and other caretaking behaviors from friends and family—naturally doses grievers with acknowledging the reality of the death. When such support is lacking or not accepted, on the other hand, grievers are more likely to remain in a perpetual state of shock. They may be living in a bubble, as it were, insulated from the truth of what happened.

In addition, grievers who are newly alone often feel anxious. This is common and understandable in the aftermath of the death of someone with whom the griever was interdependent. How will she manage without the person who died? Who or what could possibly fill the void? Where there had been a solid and important human presence, there is now only a lack. Regarding Need 6, grievers often understand on some level that they may need others to help fill the various roles vacated by the person who died, but they can't imagine how that will happen. What's more, when others reach out to them, some grievers may feel unsettled about how or if to incorporate that help into their longstanding routines. All of this may result in unease and anxiety.

Intractable sadness and depression, too, commonly indicate a dearth of grief support. A fundamental principle of my grief philosophy is that to heal, grief requires expression. It must be outwardly mourned. When it is authentically expressed, over time, its normal and natural symptoms begin to soften. By their very nature, however, sadness and depression are perhaps the largest components of the constellation of grief symptoms that some grievers tend to keep to themselves. It's often easier to share shock and anger, for example, than it is inward sadness and depression. So when grievers present with despairing sadness or depression, I know that one reason those symptoms have not eased may be that they have not yet openly shared those feelings with others.

Similarly, difficulties with trust and intimacy are often clues to an inhibition of Need 6. Personality and attachment disorders aside, grievers who aren't connected well to others are typically protecting their most vulnerable selves. Learning that it's safe to fully open themselves in your compassionate, nonjudgmental presence will help them come to appreciate the catharsis of expressing their genuine selves and truths. Inviting them to role play discussions, in which you take on the role of a friend or family member from whom they have been withholding their pain, can help them rehearse sharing with others and may embolden them to finally reach out.

Facilitating active engagement with Mourning Need 6:
Following are potential helping strategies you might employ to facilitate this mourning need.

• With appropriate timing and pacing, educate the griever about the need to receive and accept help from others. In my experience, more grievers believe that grief is their problem and theirs alone than understand that grief requires social support. As we've discussed, our culture colludes with this misconception. "I don't want to bother people," some grievers will say. Others will tell you that their family members and friends are already too busy with their own lives and problems. You can be the gentle but firm voice that emphasizes that essential mourning work is outward and social.

• As you listen to the griever's stories, make note of which friends, family members, colleagues, and others have been supportive. Also listen for times when the griever may have unknowingly rebuffed support. These clues will help you remind the griever now and then that people do care about her.

• Also listen for stories about family members and supposed friends who may be undermining or toxic to the mourning process. The griever may need suggestions about how to set boundaries with such people.

- While complicated grievers are best suited to individual therapy, sometimes participating in a grief support group provides a helpful complement to your care. It's important that support groups are a good fit because if they aren't, the experience may further complicate the already complicated grief. You can help the griever discern whether the group may be suitable for him and whether or not it has a healthy dynamic. I am an advocate of grief support groups, but I recommend them only with careful discernment for select complicated grievers.

- With the griever's permission and buy-in, suggest that the griever invite one or two others—or the entire family—to attend a session with the griever. The purpose might be to educate about and affirm the griever's naturally complicated needs as well as get everyone working toward the best interests of the griever and an understanding of how they may be able to help.

- Once you've discerned which kinds of social interactions feel most comfortable and connecting to a unique griever, offer up suggestions about ways to build more of those kinds of interactions into her days. While complicated grievers do need support specifically for their grief, they also need, as all of us do, bonds of love and friendship. Not everyone in their social or family circles will be equipped to help them with their grief, and that's OK. As long as they have you plus one or two others whom they can reliably turn to as needed with their thoughts and feelings about the loss, the remainder of their social connections will serve to strengthen the bonds that will make life worth living again.

Need 6 questions to ask yourself as you work with each unique griever:

- What is this person teaching me about what is complicating his capacity to receive and accept support from others?

- Which specific relationship issues, circumstances surrounding the death (such as stigmatized deaths), family history, or personality issues may be complicating this need?

- What are this griever's beliefs about the ability of and need for others to help him?

- Who in this griever's life is a healing helper? Who is neutral when it comes to grief support? Who is toxic?

- As a search-and-rescue companion, how can I facilitate identifying and encouraging others to walk alongside this griever on her difficult journey?

- Are there support groups in the area that might be appropriate for this griever? What about online forums or support groups that may be specific to his type of loss?

- What can I as a companion do or be for this person to create a safe place to work on this need?

The importance of the six central needs of mourning

I can't overemphasize the importance of how you, as a search-and-rescue complicated grief companion, can benefit from a working knowledge of these six needs of mourning. Essentially, dosing grievers with them is your job description. As you follow each unique griever's lead in encountering these needs, providing a safe place for their expression, you will, over time, be privileged to witness the softening of complicated grievers' symptoms.

As you become a more experienced companion, you will develop instincts about which mourning needs the griever may need more encouragement to engage with at any given time. Because grief companions are griever-led, the griever will, through her symptoms, teach you what she needs help with on any given day. Often more than one mourning need is inhibited, but you can rest assured that you don't need to cover everything all at once. As long as the griever is having a genuine, supported encounter with at least one need of mourning in each session, you are helping her achieve perturbation in the wilderness of her grief. You are helping her regain divine momentum. You are helping her move forward.

Trust that engagement with the six needs of mourning is what will rescue complicated grievers from the harrowing terrain of their grief. You are not the rescuer; mourning is. But it is your professional, compassionate companionship that will facilitate the necessary mourning. What a privilege to help accompany our fellow human beings on the most challenging journeys of their lives.

The paradoxes of mourning ④⓪

Many grief treatment models emphasize the need to get the griever to move forward, but the truth is that grievers—especially complicated grievers—need to go backward before they can move forward.

Grief is by its very nature a recursive process. That means it spirals back on itself. It is repetitive. It covers the same ground more than once. In fact, it requires repetition to eventually soften and become reconciled.

Even though some grievers are described in this book as stuck in their grief, getting them unstuck often means retracing their steps. It means going backward to the specific issues that are blocking them, such as the history of the relationship and circumstances of the death.

I call the need to go backward before going forward a paradox of mourning. There are two others I have identified: grievers

WHEN GRIEF IS COMPLICATED

need to say hello to the loss and bereavement before they can begin to say goodbye to the person who died, and grievers need to befriend the darkness before they can begin to think about reentering the light. It is the active process of honoring these three truths that ultimately creates movement.

So, for some grievers with complications, there has been a lack of honoring of the three paradoxes. For more insights into this topic, I invite you to read my book *The Paradoxes of Mourning: Healing Your Grief with Three Forgotten Truths.*

Therapy duration and frequency ❸

How long and how often should you see a complicated griever?

Because I use a mourner-led orientation to helping, the course of therapy depends entirely on the unique needs of each person. I allow my 11 tenets of companioning to guide me and to remind me to be open and flexible.

Obviously, there are times when a griever's complex loss situation will right away clue you into the fact that helping them through the terrain of their complicated grief will likely be a slow and arduous process. For example, when a traumatic death causes prolonged psychic numbing or acute aftershock in the griever, you can anticipate that a deeper and deeper encounter with Need 1, acknowledging the reality of the death, may take many sessions.

By contrast, I'll sometimes companion grievers who simply need help understanding a single contribution to the complications of their grief, such as coming from a closed family system that has discouraged them from seeking the support they need and deserve. In these situations, only a few sessions may be needed to give them momentum to set off on a healthy path.

I am, however, a believer in closed-ended therapy. While it may take some time in the beginning to understand a griever's story well enough to plan an individualized course of care, when the time is right I do like to be able to share a general schedule and possible end date with grievers. What I find is that giving us a mutually understood goal and timeframe helps impart momentum and hope to the griever. I am never rushing the griever, and I am always open to revising and extending the care plan, but at the same time, my caregiving experience has shown me that the idea of "graduation" helps gives grievers the courage and tenacity they need to do the hard work they have to do.

Still, the expected timeframe to graduation will vary a great deal from griever to griever and should depend entirely on what you learn from each new person during your first few sessions. If you already know before seeing someone how many sessions you will have, you will be more inclined to want to "treat" or "fix" them instead of companion them.

As for frequency, I suggest once-a-week sessions. For grievers who are struggling to function, you might consider meeting twice a week for the first month or so.

On occasion, you will encounter a griever whose grief vital signs indicate the need for temporary hospitalization. Grievers who are not eating or sleeping or are struggling just to survive day-to-day may need inpatient care for a short time before they are stable enough to benefit from outpatient therapy.

The "new science" of grief

In the past decade, some researchers and pop-science writers have begun to claim that mourning, i.e., grief work, is not necessary and may even be harmful to healing—a stance with which I vehemently disagree. Dr. George Bonanno, a current "new science of grief" researcher and professor of clinical psychology at Columbia University Teacher's College, claims that resiliency is the most natural and prevalent response to loss and that even after a traumatic loss, many people do not grieve deeply and those who do often recover quickly. His "empirical research" demonstrates that minimal grief is common and healthy. In my view, this stance essentially normalizes absent or carried grief.

Dr. Bonanno does allow that a minority of people, the unresilient, suffer "chronic dysfunction" in grief.

While it is outside the purview of this book to engage in an extended refutation of the new science of grief, I will just reiterate here that grief, like love, is a spiritual journey that defies measurement. From decades of professional experience I know that repeated engagement with the six needs of mourning helps people heal and that almost always, those who purport to be experiencing minimal grief after a significant loss are suppressing or denying their truth. Yes, some people are more resilient than others, and some form weaker attachments than others. I have also met many people who naturally incorporate work on the six needs of mourning into their daily lives. They talk about their pain and their memories, and they have ways— often already in place—of developing their self-identities and searching for meaning. They continue to work and play. The fact that they are not completely debilitated by their grief does not mean they are not grieving, nor does it mean they are not mourning.

A woman whose husband had died once came to me for grief counseling. This was not an unusual circumstance, of course, but what made her situation unusual was that she was worried she wasn't grieving enough. Her husband had died after a long illness, and after his death, she found that she was able to enjoy life more. She could travel and again take part in activities she enjoyed. She felt guilty about her happiness—a grief response I refer to as "joy-guilt," on page 93. During our conversation it became clear to me she was not just joyful, though—she also grieved and mourned. Even as she reveled in some aspects of her new life, she was also working on and through her grief. Yet she was resilient. I saw her once a year for several years because she appreciated the affirmation of these "grief check-ups."

As it happened, this woman was not experiencing unembarked or off-trail grief, but many grievers do. I worry that the new science of grief colludes with the societal forces that encourage the stuffing of emotionality and the carrying of grief. What's more, its scientific posturing belies the spiritual nature of love, grief, and mourning. In the throes of the technological age, I know it's tempting to want to rely on science and technology, but the hard sciences have little to teach us about what is better thought of as the "old art" of grief.

"Stuckness" and divine momentum

Many times in this book I have used the term "stuck" to describe the defining problem of complicated grief. That is, due to their unique challenges, complicated grievers often run up against a thought or a feeling or a need to behave in a certain way that is so overpowering that they get wholly caught up in it. From a mourning standpoint, they get stuck in it, like a hiker in mud. It's generally not that their thought, feeling, or behavior is wrong or bad. More commonly, it's that their thought, feeling, or behavior is more pronounced and debilitating than when that same thought, feeling, or behavior is encountered in normal grief, and furthermore, it is unchanging.

So if complicated grievers get stuck, how do they get unstuck? With the grace of divine momentum. Your role is to help dose them with the pertinent six needs of mourning until they can feel themselves moving again. Divine momentum is the notion that the process of mourning naturally and necessarily leads to healing and reconciliation. In other words, every time they meet (or, because grief is recursive, re-meet) a need of mourning, grievers move forward. They experience perturbation—the movement that enables change.

As grief companion, you unleash and continue to nurture divine momentum by using your self as instrument and by leveraging your helping skills to facilitate effective encounters with the six needs of mourning.

Common complicated grief therapy mistakes

In my bereavement caregiver seminars and training classes, participants sometimes ask me if I have noticed any common complicated grief therapy mistakes. Here are a select few:

• *Entering into helping relationships with complicated grievers without understanding the distinction between grief support and grief therapy.* Please see page 137 for more on this important topic.

• *Over-normalizing to the point of missing the significance of complicating factors.* Counselors may tell grievers, "Grief is normal." And by now you know that I agree with this! But still, it is also important not to downplay the risk factors for complicated grief we reviewed in Part One. When one or more of them are present, the griever may well be experiencing complicated grief. Caregivers who lack the knowledge and skills to carry out a comprehensive initial inventory also generally lack the training and skills to help complicated grievers with their unique needs.

- *Projecting over-identification with the griever out of one's personal experience.* Therapists who have not fully integrated their own life losses may allow that reality to seep into a loss of objectivity in supporting the griever. In the helping process, you can never take anyone further than you have gone yourself.

- *Pathologizing griefbursts.* Caregivers who lack grief education and training sometimes inappropriately suggest to grievers that their intense bursts of emotion are abnormal.

- *Getting the "why" and the "how" backward.* Therapists focused on moving grievers forward often overlook the fact that before grievers can think about *how* to move forward, they first have to figure out *why* to move forward. Mourning Need 5, the search for meaning, is necessarily inward-directed before it can be outward-directed.

- *Desiring to simply learn techniques to achieve inappropriate therapeutic goals.* In other words, some therapists want to learn techniques to get complicated grievers to let go and move forward quickly and efficiently. Unfortunately, such care plans often do more harm than good.

- *Working from the belief that "one size fits all."* Manualized care plans in which every griever is prescribed the same "treatment" do not provide adequate care. There are a multitude of unique aspects to complications of grief that demand a customized approach to caregiving.

- *Not understanding that one of the most important qualities for caregivers to complicated grievers is patience.* Therapists who lack

WHEN GRIEF IS COMPLICATED

respect for grievers' natural defenses often try to push grievers to places they are not ready to go. As I always say, there are no rewards for speed, but there are many benefits to going slowly and allowing the griever to teach you the importance of timing and pacing in your helping efforts.

In enumerating mistakes, I do not mean to imply that grief companions should be perfect. I myself, especially early in my career, made some mistakes and perpetuated some grief misconceptions. But the companioning orientation asks us to be learners instead of experts. I hope you will join me in learning from our own mistakes as well as those of others so that we can provide more compassionate, effective care to the complicated grievers who need it most.

Medical-model treatments for complicated grief

Interestingly, the medical-model literature on effective treatments for complicated grief points to the efficacy of talk therapy as well.

In 2005, Dr. Katherine Shear and colleagues conducted a preliminary study comparing results of a 16-session course of interpersonal therapy (IPT) with a 16-session course of what is now termed "complicated grief treatment" (CGT).

As closed-ended programs, both included introductory, middle, and ending phases. In the introductory phase, the IPT patients disclosed their symptoms and completed an interpersonal inventory. In sessions, grievers talked about their grief, role transitions, and disputes with people in their lives, with topical direction from the therapists. The therapists also helped grievers "arrive at a more realistic assessment of the relationship with the deceased…and encouraged the pursuit of satisfying relationships and activities." In the concluding phase, patients were asked to assess treatment gains and talk about plans for the future.

In the CGT sessions, therapists more rigidly followed a treatment plan manual. Early sessions included the therapist explaining the differences between normal and complicated grief and describing the dual-process model as well as a discussion of life goals. Middle sessions required specific exposure-therapy techniques such as the griever closing her eyes and telling the story of the death. The story was recorded, and the patient was asked to listen to the recording at home throughout the next week. Patients were also asked to have imagined conversations with the deceased (including answering as the deceased), complete memory questionnaires (including both good and bad memories), and take part in other exercises.

This small-scale study determined that the more regimented CGT protocol produced marginally better results than the IPT model, measured with inventory tools assessing things such as depression, anxiety, and work and social adjustment.

Since then, CGT protocols have been further studied and refined to include additional exposure therapy and cognitive behavioral therapy techniques. A number of therapists and grief programs now use a CGT manualized model consisting of 16 45-to-60-minute structured sessions. In between the guided sessions—which are a blend of IPT, CBT, and motivational interviewing—patients are asked to complete exercises at home, such as a daily grief monitoring diary, at-home repetition of in-session exercises, and restorative activities (in keeping with the dual-process, or evade-encounter, model). Several recent studies have shown good results and demonstrate that this regimen may be more effective than IPT alone, as measured by lower levels of avoidance of the loss, lower levels of guilt, and fewer negative thoughts about the future.

At Dr. Shear's Center for Complicated Grief, therapists use this lockstep 16-session model, stating that it "guides people in resolving grief complications and revitalizes the natural healing process." Their CGT system includes seven core modules, which are introduced during the first six sessions and called upon in various ways in the remaining ten sessions.

- Grief and treatment information

- Emotional self-monitoring and self-regulation

- Long-term goals development

- Social network development

- Reflections on the death and sharing those reflections

- Exposure to places and situations that evoke reminders of the loss

- Memories of the person who died—accessing and fostering a continued connection

I agree that it is often effective to incorporate all seven of these goals and activities into a therapeutic treatment plan for complicated grievers. In fact, you might notice that these goals correlate closely with the six needs of mourning:

- Grief and treatment information (Need 1: Acknowledge the reality)

- Emotional self-monitoring and self-regulation (Need 2: Embrace the pain)

- Long-term goals development (Need 4: Develop a new self-identity and Need 5: Search for meaning)

- Social network development (Need 6: Receive and accept support from others)

- Reflections on the death and sharing those reflections (All the needs)

- Exposure to places and situations that evoke reminders of the loss (Need 1: Acknowledge the reality and Need 3: Remember the person who died)

- Memories of the person who died—accessing and fostering a continued connection (Need 3: Remember the person who died)

In other words, as I have already reviewed, I agree that dosing complicated grievers in a safe, bonded, therapeutic environment with the six needs of mourning is the only effective "treatment." We're basically on the same page! Besides our fundamental disagreement that grief can be scientifically assessed and measured (I strongly believe grief therapy is more art than science), where I part company with the CGT medical model is in the labeling of complicated grief as a form of mental illness and in the therapist-led delivery of rigid, session-by-session therapeutic tools and techniques. What's more, manualized therapies tend to position the therapist as the expert and the griever as the subordinate. Therapists are at risk for projecting a superior knowledge of the griever's experience, when in fact the griever is the expert and the therapist the learner.

As a search-and-rescue companion, you will meet the complicated grievers in your care in a limitless variety of circumstances and with widely varying care-eliciting symptoms and challenges. As a result, each of them needs and deserves highly individualized care.

Some grievers do not need help with memory work in general because they're doing it on their own but could really use support in reviewing one or two particularly troubling memories. Others seem to be plugged into a solid social network, generally speaking, but are having trouble with a certain family member. Some are mostly angry; they need help understanding and working through their anger. Others have multiple losses to work on. Some speak with great zeal about their faith and global meaning-related beliefs but have trouble getting out of bed in the morning.

Any generic, manualized treatment plan, even one that encourages therapists to use their judgment in adjusting the plan to the needs of the individual griever, is likely to miss the mark a great deal of the time. Meanwhile, the griever's most pronounced symptoms and issues are likely to be under-attended-to. Still, I can also see that regardless of these limitations, the process of participating in 16 sessions of manualized grief therapy will help many grievers work through at least some of their challenges and feel both supported and validated in their need for support. Talking openly and honestly about grief and struggles with loss in the presence of a compassionate therapist is almost always a win.

What's more, I understand the attraction of a manualized, time-limited therapy process for complicated grief. It gives therapists a structure and detailed to-do list for every hour they spend with a griever. On the griever's side of the equation, it provides a set timeframe and a checklist: do these things, this many times, and you'll feel better. If only it were so simple!

I also know that we have a great need for higher numbers of trained complicated grief companions. I'll be talking about my own complicated grief caregiver training course later in this section, but of course, I don't have the capacity to train as many therapists as the world needs. And the world needs all the help it can get.

If you are a CGT therapist, I urge you to try thinking of CGT as one important tool in your toolkit. Perhaps my companioning model can be another. It's always useful to glean understanding from more than one tradition or model, and the more open you are to trying various approaches (within reason), the more likely you are to have at the ready a variety of tools and techniques that you can call upon as needed for any given griever in your care.

Pharmacotherapy for complicated grief 22

I believe that grief is a normal existential experience of the heart and soul—the necessary twin of love. But is it also possible that drug therapy can be a responsible part of a complicated grief companioning plan?

First, let's take a look at the research. A 2016 study found that 16 sessions of complicated-grief-specific psychotherapy was significantly more effective at producing global improvement than treatment with the antidepressant citalopram, though depression and suicidal ideation in the context of grief were significantly eased by a combination of both therapies. Other, earlier studies suggested that antidepressants may enable grievers to better encounter their painful memories and exposure-therapy exercises. One 2007 study even suggested that SSRIs alone may be sufficient to treat complicated grief. And a two-year study, now underway, is looking at whether or not an oxytocin nasal spray could be used to treat away symptoms of complicated grief. Results have not yet been published.

Obviously, I would never support a pharmacological "cure" for complicated grief any more than I would support a "cure" for love. Any chemical agent used to completely remove a human's emotional and spiritual highs and lows is only suited for dystopian fiction, in my opinion. People are made to feel, and feelings have profound purposes.

Yet there is absolutely a role for antidepressants and perhaps other pharmacological agents in helping support grievers on their journeys. As mentioned earlier, it is true that grievers affected by clinical depression, post-traumatic stress, and other acute symptoms often need pharmacological support to be functional enough to work on the six needs of mourning. While pain and anxiety are natural and functional parts of the grief journey, when they become overwhelming or all-consuming, they are no longer functional. Interestingly, I run across some caregivers who believe that antidepressants inhibit the capacity to actively mourn. I disagree. The medication, when indicated, can create the energy to convert grief into mourning.

Still, I urge you to use your professional discernment as well as understanding of the companioning approach to grief care in guiding grievers' use of medication and supplements. There can be a fine line between treating debilitating chemical imbalances and eradicating or self-treating necessary grief.

Family counseling for complicated grief 44

I have found that the use of a family systems approach with complicated grief is essential to the helping process. My experience suggests that the people who would usually be the strongest source of support, or Mourning Need 6, to grievers—their immediate family members—are often the most exposed to and thus frightened by the intensity, severity, and duration of the grievers' symptoms. This situation can result in an even more profound sense of loss and isolation for complicated grievers, who often feel that family and friends do not really understand what they are experiencing.

To understand a particular griever's needs, we must understand the systems in which she exists: the culture, the community, and most importantly, the family. The caregiver who receives training in a family perspective sees human beings as "belonging to something." The core" thing" to which they belong is most often (though not always) a large group of people. A family. Sometimes the griever belongs to an open–family system that acknowledges death and encourages authentic mourning. Other times it is a closed-family system that shuts down and essentially says, verbally or nonverbally, "We don't do death." The quality of the family environment (and rules surrounding death, grief, and mourning) is a major influence on the griever's capacity to mourn in healthy ways. It only makes good sense that if the family system is a central complication of the griever's journey, you as companion must try to work with the family.

Family-oriented grief therapy integrates family members into the therapy process. This is not to suggest that the entire family must be present for all counseling sessions. On the contrary, I would recommend having an initial family session early on in the counseling process and then move family members in and out of sessions depending on the unique needs that evolve over time. It may also be appropriate for you to suggest additional individual counseling to others in the family. Ironically, in my professional experience it is the "identified patient" who is often the one with the best self-awareness and most effective mourning skills in the group.

Overall, your goals in working with the family are to create a safe place to encounter the six needs of mourning, to help the family understand grief and complicated grief, to provide an outside perspective, to help family members understand one another's behaviors and feelings, to clarify discrepancies in communication within the family, to delineate changed roles within the family, to build self-esteem and self-efficacy, to facilitate ritual as a means of healing, to act as family advocate, to validate all family members for the courage to mourn, and to provide hope for healing.

What to do when you don't know what to do

As you work to develop your knowledge and experience with complicated grief, I urge you to identify and secure mentors who can be available for your supervision and ongoing support of your helping efforts. These are professionals—I call them "responsibility partners"—you can turn to when you don't know what to do with a particular complication or griever. It is always wise to consult with another experienced counselor. In addition, working with complicated grief demands the ability to monitor how this work impacts you. You are at risk for vicarious traumatization, and part of your self-care should include regular debriefing.

As we discussed earlier, it is important to discern up front if your training, background, and experience are an appropriate match for a given griever. However, sometimes you will not know until after you've entered into a therapeutic relationship with a griever that you need to refer him to a caregiver with more advanced or specialized training. My most frequent referral over the years has been grievers abusing or dependent on drugs or alcohol. I have referred them for chemical abuse/dependence treatment prior to companioning them for complicated grief.

A potential challenge is finding sources of referral. Why? Because I believe we have more people struggling with complications of grief than we have people trained to help them. Having acknowledged this challenge, I suggest you look at the Association of Death Education and Counseling's referral network, which you'll find at www.adec.org.

Reconciliation in grief 41

Our goal in companioning complicated grievers is to help them return to a healthy path and good momentum in the wilderness of their grief. They are either stuck or off-trail (or both), and they simply need help to get moving again.

But when, with your companionship, they are able to get moving and on track again, what is the destination of their journey? In other words, how will you know when the complicated griever in your care is safely through the most treacherous terrain? Or, if you will not be companioning the griever long enough to discern this, what hope can you offer the griever for his eventual life?

A number of the grief thinkers and researchers we have mentioned in this book think of the "end point" of grief as resolution, recovery, reestablishment, or reorganization. It is often seen as a return to "normalcy." Yet the truth is that grief changes people forever. For the griever to assume that life will return to "normal," as it was before the death, is unrealistic and potentially damaging.

Reconciliation is a term I believe to be more apt for what occurs as the griever works to integrate the new reality of moving forward in life without the physical presence of the person who has died. What occurs is a renewed sense of energy and confidence, an ability to fully acknowledge the reality of the death, and the capacity to become reinvolved in the activities of living. Also an acknowledgment occurs that pain and grief are difficult yet necessary parts of life.

As the experience of reconciliation unfolds, the griever recognizes that life will be different without the presence of the significant person who died. A realization occurs that reconciliation is a process, not an event. Working through the emotional relationship with the person who died and redirecting energy and initiative toward the future often take longer and involve more labor than most people are aware. We as human beings never "get over" our grief but instead become reconciled to it.

In reconciliation, the loss becomes an integrated part of the griever's life. Beyond an intellectual working through is an emotional and spiritual working through. What had been understood at the "head level" is now understood at the "heart level." When reminders such as holidays, anniversaries, or other special memories are triggered, the griever experiences the intense pain of grief, yet the duration is typically shorter as the healing of reconciliation occurs.

The pain of grief goes from being ever-present, sharp, and stinging to an acknowledged feeling of loss that has given rise to renewed meaning and purpose. The sense of loss does not completely disappear yet softens, and the intense pangs of grief become less frequent. Hope for a continued life emerges as the griever is able to make commitments to the future, realizing that the dead person will never be forgotten, yet knowing that one's own life can and will move forward.

For the companion, establishing the hope of eventual reconciliation in the griever is essential. Most grievers but especially complicated grievers experience a loss of confidence and self-esteem that leaves them questioning their capacity to heal. Companions who are able to supportively embrace a willingness to hope and to anticipate reconciliation assist mourners in movement toward their grief instead of away from it.

Just as we expect that grievers experience pain as a part of reconciliation, when we expect reconciliation, and we know it is possible, we help the person acknowledge reconciliation as a realistic hope. However, if we as helpers somehow collaborate with grievers who perceive that they will never move beyond the acute pain of their grief, we may well become a hindrance to their eventual healing.

Just as grief is normal, reconciliation of grief is normal. Yet grievers need support, especially complicated grievers, as well as compassion, patience, perseverance, determination, and, perhaps most of all, hope and the belief in their capacity to heal. Part of your helping role is to serve as a catalyst that creates conditions outside the person and qualities within the person that make healing possible.

As you work to support the reconciliation process, you do not impose your own direction on the content of what is explored; rather, you allow the direction of the griever's experience to guide what you do and to help determine how you respond in supportive, life-enhancing ways. You appreciate the person as being independent from you and respect his right to determine the direction of the companioning relationship.

Signs of reconciliation

When I companion grievers, I never seek to hurry them along, I allow them to proceed at their own pace, but I do watch for the following signs that they may be on the downhill side of their journey through the wilderness.

Note that not every person will demonstrate all of these signs. However, the majority of the signs should be present for the griever to be considered in the reconciliation phase of the journey. I have seen that many grievers try to convince themselves and others that they are further along in the healing process than they actually are. You can help by reminding that the griever that there are no rewards for speed.

- A recognition of the reality and finality of the death, in both the head and the heart.

- A return to stable and ideally healthy eating and sleeping patterns.

- A renewed sense of energy and personal well-being.

- A subjective sense of release or relief from the person who died. The griever still has thoughts of and feelings for the person but isn't preoccupied with these thoughts and feelings.

- The capacity to enjoy experiences in life that should normally be enjoyable.

- The establishment of new and healthy relationships.

WHEN GRIEF IS COMPLICATED

- The capacity to live a full life without feelings of guilt or lack of self-respect.

- The capacity to organize and plan one's life toward the future.

- The capacity to become comfortable with the way things are rather than attempting to make things as they were.

- The capacity to being open to more change in one's life.

- The awareness that one has allowed oneself to fully mourn and has survived.

- The awareness that one does not "get over" grief but instead acknowledges that, "This is my new reality, and I am ultimately the one who must work to create new meaning and purpose in my life."

- The capacity to acknowledge new parts of one's life that have been discovered in the growth through ones grief.

- The capacity to adjust to the new role changes that have resulted from the loss of the relationship.

- The capacity to be compassionate with oneself when normal griefbursts arise, such as on holidays, anniversaries, and other special occasions.

- The capacity to acknowledge that the pain of loss is an inherent part of life that results from the ability to give and receive love.

There is nothing more professionally rewarding to me than when a complicated griever I have been companioning begins to demonstrate signs of reconciliation. The signs are often quite subtle at first, and backsliding may occur now and then in between sessions, but eventually they become more pronounced and I know that the griever has made it safely through the most harrowing stage of the journey.

Earlier I said that I am a proponent of closed-ended therapy. I have found that the idea of graduation from therapy—even in the early days, when it may seem like a far-off goal—helps grievers believe they can and will begin to feel better one day. And when that day arrives, they, too, are able to recognize it. We have been noting their progress all along, and they can see the difference.

With complicated grievers who are ready to graduate from my care, I sometimes help them create a self-care plan that continues the work we have done together. The plan gives them ongoing permission to take good care of themselves as they continue to grieve and declares mourning strategies that they like and that have proven to work for them in our time together.

I also like to suggest follow-up visits. Check-ups, if you will. We might meet three months after graduation, then six months after that, then a year after that, with annual check-ups after that if desired. Because grief never ends, and because complicated grief is more prone to severe griefbursting and possible recidivism down the line, especially when other losses or significant life challenges arise, annual check-ups are a good standard of care.

Complicated grief therapy training recommendations

Advanced training for complicated grief therapists is not widely available, but I have listed below the training options I am aware of.

At my Companioning Institute for Grief Caregivers, I teach a 4-day training on complicated grief companioning several times a year. You can find details at www.centerforloss.com.

Dr. Katherine Shear's Center for Complicated Grief, at the

Columbia School of Social Work, in New York, New York, offers a number of one- and two-day training sessions on various aspects of complicated grief therapy at beginner, intermediate, and advanced levels. You can find details at www.complicatedgrief.columbia.edu.

The American Association of Suicidology offers a one-day Suicide Bereavement Clinician Training Program. You can find details at www.suicidiology.org.

Dr. Therese Rando has created a video training program entitled "Core Strategies for Treating Traumatic Bereavement." You can find details at www.jkseminars.com.

And finally, the Association for Death Education and Counseling, or ADEC, offers various resources, including certifications, conferences, webinars, and more. You can find details at www.adec.org.

Self-care for complicated grief therapists

For therapist companions to complicated grievers, good self-companionship is critical for at least three major reasons.

First and most important, we owe it to ourselves and our families to lead joyful, whole lives. While companioning grievers is certainly rewarding, we cannot and should not expect our work to fulfill us completely.

Second, our work is draining—physically, emotionally, and spiritually. Assisting bereaved people is a demanding interpersonal process that requires a great deal of energy and focus. Whenever we attempt to respond to the needs of those in grief, chances are slim that we can (or should) avoid the stress of emotional involvement. Each day we open ourselves to caring about the bereaved and their personal life journeys. And genuinely caring about people and their families—especially those affected by some of the most traumatic loss circumstances—touches the depths of our hearts and souls. We need relief from such draining work.

And third, we owe it to grievers themselves. My personal experience and observation suggest that good self-companionship is an essential foundation of caring about grievers. They are sensitive to our ability to "be with" them. Poor self-care results in distraction from the helping relationship, and grieving people often intuit when we are not physically, emotionally, and spiritually available to them.

Sometimes caregivers who practice poor self-companionship also distance themselves from others' pain by taking on the stance of the "expert." Because many of us have been trained to remain professionally distant, we may stay aloof from the very people we are supposed to help. Generally, this is a projection of our own need to stay removed from the pain of others as well as from our own life hurts. Yet the expert mode is antithetical to compassionate care, and can cause an irreparable rift between you and those you are honored to companion.

So, does this work have to be exhausting? Naturally, draining, yes, but exhausting? I don't think so. Yes, good helpers naturally focus outward, resulting in a drain on both head and heart. And yes, you will hear some people say, "If you do this kind of caregiving, you might as well resign yourself to eventually burning out." Again, I don't think so. I have been doing it for four decades and can honestly say I feel so blessed to do what I do to help my fellow human beings each and every day. I hope you can say the same.

For complicated grief therapists, the key to preventing burnout and secondary traumatization is to practice daily, ongoing, nurturing self-companionship, including reciprocating mentorship and debriefing with professional responsibility partners. While detailed self-care tips and guidelines are outside the purview of this book, I urge you also to look into my book *Companioning You! A Soulful Guide to Caring for Yourself While You Care for the Dying and the Bereaved*, which explores readers' understanding of their own caregiving styles and risks for burnout then offers a step-by-step, eight-week self-companioning reset.

I hope this how-to section is helpful to you in your work companioning people experiencing complicated grief. As you gain more experience, I encourage you to continue to learn and try new tools that facilitate active work on the six needs of mourning with the complicated grievers in your care. As long as you are ascribing to the companioning tenets, using appropriate timing and pacing, and allowing each unique griever's current strengths and challenges to guide your recommendations, any technique that helps grievers encounter inhibited mourning needs may be helpful. Remember to go slowly. In each session, there are no rewards for speed. You are not attached to outcome. And you always remain hopeful for and ready to affirm divine momentum.

Questions for reflection and understanding

In a blank notebook or computer file, I invite you to answer the provided questions. Writing down your thoughts will help you understand and remember the concepts as well as integrate them with your unique methods of helping grievers.

• Which vital signs do you check for when you meet with grievers?

• How do you provide shelter to the grievers in your care?

• What do you think sustains complicated grievers during the therapy process and why?

• Describe the tools in your companioning toolkit.

• Where do you see yourself on the continuum of grief counselor to grief therapist? What are your strengths? What are your possible limitations?

• In your training, what did you learn about curing mental-health conditions? How do those concepts apply to grief care?

- How do you feel about the self-as-instrument caregiving philosophy and why?

- Of the essential ingredients for complicated grief companions listed on pages 132 to 139, which are among your strengths? Which do you struggle with?

- Do you agree that mourning—the active, outward expression of grief—helps grievers heal? Why or why not?

- Describe your work with complicated grievers to date and how your caring strategies have been different from and similar to the four-step companioning model for complicated grief.

- What do you believe about the concept of grief work, especially as the path to healing?

- What successes and challenges have you experienced in your practice related to grievers' encounters with Mourning Need 1?

- What successes and challenges have you experienced in your practice related to grievers' encounters with Mourning Need 2?

- What successes and challenges have you experienced in your practice related to grievers' encounters with Mourning Need 3?

- What successes and challenges have you experienced in your practice related to grievers' encounters with Mourning Need 4?

- What successes and challenges have you experienced in your practice related to grievers' encounters with Mourning Need 5?

- What successes and challenges have you experienced in your practice related to grievers' encounters with Mourning Need 6?

- How do you educate about and facilitate grievers' needs to vacillate between encountering their grief and evading their grief?

- How do you incorporate grief education in general into your complicated grief care plans?

- Describe your experiences to date working with traumatized grievers, including successes, challenges, and questions.

- Jot down any rituals you use to prepare for each therapy session.

- What do you think are good guidelines for therapy duration and frequency for complicated grievers?

- What is your opinion of the "new science" of grief?

- Explain your understanding of stuckness and divine momentum in grief.

- What mistakes have you made or seen in complicated grief care?

- Do you have training in or experience with medical-model-based complicated grief treatment? What do you think is effective about this model? What is ineffective?

- Provide an example of a time when medication was helpful to a griever in helping him create momentum in his journey. If you've ever seen medication used inappropriately, describe that as well.

- Do you have experience in using family counseling for complicated grief? If so, how has it worked for you? If not, how do you feel about incorporating it when appropriate?

- Describe the network of mentors and responsibility partners you turn to when you need to discuss professional challenges, debrief, and/or refer.

- Which signs have you most often noticed in grievers who are beginning to achieve some degree of reconciliation of their grief? Give examples.

- Have you received training for complicated grief therapy? Where, when, and what did you think of it?

- What are your self-care strengths and challenges right now?

- Do you have any other thoughts, comments, or questions about how to companion complicated grievers?

A Final Word

As I have said and written many times, "We do not need to be joined at the head with a griever; we need to be joined at the heart." I believe this is never more true than when we are companioning those who are experiencing complicated grief.

The transformation of our culture into one that embraces grief and mourning as natural and necessary parts of human life is my vision. Learning from my own grief and those I have had the honor of working with is my passion and my purpose. I hope you have found this primer useful as you work to understand complicated grief and the art of companioning those in need of your caregiving efforts. Please consider writing or emailing me your reflections and any questions you might have about this critically important topic (DrWolfelt@centerforloss.com).

My hope and my dream is that together, we can be a force for positive change in the grief-avoiding culture we live in. Let's keep learning from each other and work to create safe, sacred spaces for people to mourn well so they can live well and love well. Let's keep making bereavement care better. Let's be a force for positive change, both in the lives of individuals and families and in our society as a whole.

Now I suggest you take the rest of the day off, go out into nature, and have gratitude for the gift of life you have been given. And as you do this, remember the wise words of St. Catherine of Siena: "When we are whom we are called to be, we will set the world ablaze."

Bibliography

Boerner, Kathrin, and Richard Schulz. "Caregiving, Bereavement, and Complicated Grief," in *Bereavement Care*, 28(3) (December 2009): 10-13.

Bonanno, George A. *The Other Side of Sadness: What the New Science of Bereavement Tells Us About Life After Loss.* New York: Basic Books, 2009.

Bowlby, John. *Attachment and Loss, Vol. 3.* First edition. New York: Basic Books, 1981.

Diagnostic and Statistical Manual of Mental Disorders, Fifth edition, DSM-5. American Washington, DC: Psychiatric Association Publishing, 2013.

Doka, Kenneth J., ed. *Disenfranchised Grief: New Directions, Challenges, and Strategies for Practice.* Champaign, Illinois: Research Press, 2002.

Gentile, Julie P. "Pathological Grief," in ed. Jerald Kay, *Hospital Physician Psychiatry Board Review Manual*, Volume 8, Part 1. Wayne, Pennsylvania: Turner White Communications, 2004.

Jancin, Bruce. "Complicated Grief Treatment Gets Better Results than Interpersonal Psychotherapy," in *Clinical Psychiatry News*, May 26, 2017.

Jordan, John R. and Robert A. Neimeyer, "Historical and Contemporary Perspectives on Assessment and Intervention," Chapter 21 in eds. David K. Meagher and David E. Balk, *The Handbook of Thanatology*. Second Edition. Abingdon, England: Routledge, 2013.

Klass Dennis, Phyllis Silverman, and Steven Nickman , eds. *Continuing Bonds: New Understandings of Grief.* Washington: Taylor & Francis, 1996.

Maciejewski, Paul K., Andreas Maercker, Paul A. Boelen, Holly G. Prigerson, "'Prolonged Grief Disorder' and 'Persistent Complex Bereavement Disorder,' but Not 'Complicated Grief,' Are One and the Same Diagnostic Entity: An Analysis of Data from the Yale Bereavement Study," in *World Psychiatry,* 15(3) (October 2016).

Marzillier, John. *The Trauma Therapies*. Oxford, England: Oxford University Press, 2014.

O'Connor, Mary-Frances, and Brian J. Arizmendi. "Neuropsychological Correlates of Complicated Grief in Older Spousally Bereaved Adults," in *The Journals of Gerontology: Series B, Psychological Sciences and Social Sciences*, 69B(1) (January 2014): 12-18.

Parkes, Colin Murray. *Bereavement: Studies in Grief in Adult Life*. London: Tavistock, 1972.

Pearlman, Laurie Anne, Camille B. Wortman, Catherine A. Feuer, Christine H. Farber, and Therese A. Rando. *Treating Traumatic Bereavement: A Practitioner's Guide*. New York: The Guilford Press, 2014.

Rando, Therese A. *Treatment of Complicated Mourning*. Champaign, Illinois: Research Press, 1993.

Shear, Katherine, Timothy Monk, Patricia Houck, Nadine Melhem, Ellen Frank, Charles Reynolds, Russell Sillowash. "An Attachment-based Model of Complicated Grief Including the Role of Avoidance." *European Archives of Psychiatry and Clinical Neuroscience* 257(8) (December 2007): 453-461.

Shear, Katherine M. "Complicated Grief," in *The New England Journal of Medicine*, 372 (January 8, 2015): 153-160.

Shear, Katherine M. et al. "Complicated Grief and Related Bereavement Issues for DSM-5," in *Depression and Anxiety*, 28(2) (February 2011): 103-117.

Shear, Katherine M. *Complicated Grief Treatment: Instruction Manual used in NIMH Grants*. New York: Columbia Center for Complicated Grief, Columbia University, 2015.

Shear, Katherine M., Ellen Frank, Patricia Houck, et al. "Treatment of Complicated Grief: A Randomized Controlled Trial," in *Journal of the American Medical Association*, 293(21) (2005): 2601-2608.

Simon, Naomi M., E.H. Thompson, M.H. Pollack, and Katherine M. Shear, "Complicated Grief: A Case Series Using Escitalopram," in *American Journal of Psychiatry*, 164 (2007): 1760–1761.

Simon, Naomi M., Katherine M. Shear, A. Fagiolini, Ellen Frank, A. Zalta, E.H. Thompson, C.F. Reynolds 3rd, and Russell Sillowash. "Impact of Concurrent Naturalistic Pharmacotherapy on Psychotherapy of Complicated Grief," in *Psychiatry Research* 159(1-2) (May 30, 2008): 31-36.

Stroebe, Margaret, and Henk Schut. "The Dual-Process Model of Coping with Bereavement: Rationale and Description." *Death Studies* 23 (1999): 197-224.

Volpe, Andrea. "Is Grief a Disease?" in *The Atlantic*, November 16, 2016.

Wagner, Birgit and Andreas Maercker. "The Diagnosis of Complicated Grief as a Mental Disorder: A Critical Appraisal," in *Psychologica Belgica*, 50(1&2) (2010): 27-48.

Wetherell, Julie Loebach. "Complicated Grief Therapy as a New Treatment Approach," in *Dialogues in Clinical Neuroscience*, 14(2) (June 2012): 159-166.

Wolfelt, Alan D. *Companioning the Bereaved: A Soulful Guide for Caregivers*. Fort Collins, Colorado: Companion Press, 2006.

Wolfelt, Alan D. *Companioning You! A Soulful Guide to Caring for Yourself While You Care for the Dying and the Bereaved*. Fort Collins, Colorado: Companion Press, 2012.

Wolfelt, Alan D. *Counseling Skills for Companioning the Mourner: The Fundamentals of Effective Grief Counseling*. Fort Collins, Colorado: Companion Press, 2016.

Wolfelt, Alan D. *Reframing PTSD as Traumatic Grief: How Caregivers Can Companion Traumatized Grievers Through Catch-Up Mourning*. Fort Collins, Colorado: Companion Press, 2014.

Worden, William J. *Grief Counseling and Grief Therapy: A Handbook for the Mental Health Practitioner*. Fourth edition. New York: Springer Publishing Company, 2008.

Complicated Grief
EDUCATIONAL
SUPPLEMENT

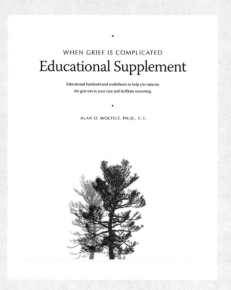

If you're companioning complicated grievers, this packet contains dozens of educational handouts and worksheets to help you educate the grievers in your care and facilitate mourning. Simply purchase and download the supplement PDF at **www.centerforloss.com** and print out individual sheets as needed.

The handouts and worksheets are number coded for easy cross-referencing with the content of *When Grief is Complicated*.

50-page PDF • $19.95

Companion
PRESS

All publications can be ordered by mail from:

Companion Press
3735 Broken Bow Road
Fort Collins, CO 80526
Phone: (970) 226-6050
Fax: 1-800-922-6051
www.centerforloss.com

Complicated Grief Educational Supplement list of contents

Presentations, Trainings, and Consultations by Dr. Wolfelt

To contact Dr. Wolfelt about speaking engagements or training opportunities at his Companioning Institute for Grief Caregivers, visit www.centerforloss.com, call 970.226.6050, or email him at DrWolfelt@centerforloss.com.

If you are a grief companion who would like to arrange a potential phone consultation with Dr. Wolfelt about the care of a complicated griever or other professional matter, please call the Center for Loss at 970.226.6050.

In Gratitude

We extend our gratitude to Operation Family Fund for providing a grant to assist with the creation of this book.

Ten percent of net revenues from sales of *When Grief is Complicated* will be donated back to Operation Family Fund in support of their mission, which is to assist US military members and civilians severely disabled during Operation Enduring and Iraqi Freedom, as well as their families and caregivers, in achieving financial self-sufficiency and finding solutions to short- and long-term needs.

Operation Family Fund is a private non-profit 501 (c)(3) charitable organization funded by private donations and run by volunteers.

To learn more and to support Operation Family Fund, please contact:

Operation Family Fund
PO Box 837
Ridgecrest, CA 93556
www.operationfamilyfund.org

ALAN D. WOLFELT, PH.D.

Companioning the Bereaved
A Soulful Guide for Caregivers

This book by one of North America's most respected grief educators presents a model for grief counseling based on his "companioning" principles.

For many mental healthcare providers, grief in contemporary society has been medicalized—perceived as if it were an illness that with proper assessment, diagnosis, and treatment could be cured.

Dr. Wolfelt explains that our modern understanding of grief all too often conveys that at bereavement's "end" the mourner has completed a series of tasks, extinguished pain, and established new relationships. Our psychological models emphasize "recovery" or "resolution" in grief, suggesting a return to "normalcy."

By contrast, this book advocates a model of "companioning" the bereaved, acknowledging that grief forever changes or transforms the mourner's world view. Companioning is not about assessing, analyzing, fixing, or resolving another's grief. Instead, it is about being totally present to the mourner, even being a temporary guardian of his soul. The companioning model is grounded in a "teach me" perspective.

"This outstanding book should be required reading for each and every grief provider. Dr. Wolfelt's philosophy and practice of caregiving helps us understand we don't need to be joined at the head with the mourner, we need to be joined at the heart."

— A GRIEF COUNSELOR

ISBN 978-1-879651-41-8 • 191 pages • hardcover • $29.95

Companion
PRESS

All publications can be ordered by mail from:

Companion Press
3735 Broken Bow Road
Fort Collins, CO 80526
Phone: (970) 226-6050
Fax: 1-800-922-6051
www.centerforloss.com

Companioning the Grieving Child
A Soulful Guide for Caregivers

Renowned author and educator Dr. Alan Wolfelt redefines the role of the grief counselor in this guide for caregivers to grieving children. Providing a viable alternative to the limitations of the medical establishment's model for companioning the bereaved, Dr. Wolfelt encourages counselors and other caregivers to aspire to a more compassionate philosophy in which the child is the expert of his or her grief—not the counselor or caregiver. The approach outlined in the book argues against treating grief as an illness to be diagnosed and treated but rather for acknowledging it as an experience that forever changes a child's worldview. By promoting careful listening and observation, this guide shows caregivers, family members, teachers, and others how to support grieving children and help them grow into healthy adults.

ISBN 978-1-61722-158-3 • 160 pages • hardcover • $29.95

Companion
P R E S S

All publications can be ordered by mail from:

Companion Press

3735 Broken Bow Road
Fort Collins, CO 80526

Phone: (970) 226-6050
Fax: 1-800-922-6051

www.centerforloss.com

The Companioning the Grieving Child Curriculum Book
Activities to Help Children and Teens Heal

BY PATRICIA MORRISSEY, M.S. ED.

FOREWORD BY ALAN D. WOLFELT, PH.D.

Based on Dr. Wolfelt's six needs of mourning and written to pair with Companioning the Grieving Child, this comprehensive guide provides hundreds of hands-on activities tailored for grieving children in three age groups: preschool, elementary, and teens. Through the use of readings, games, discussion questions, and arts and crafts, counselors will help grieving young people acknowledge the reality of the death, embrace the pain of the loss, remember the person who died, develop a new self-identity, search for meaning, and accept support from others.

Sample activities include:

• Grief sock puppets

• Tissue paper butterflies in conjunction with the picture book My, Oh My—A Butterfly!

• Expression bead bracelets

• The nurturing game

• Write an autobiopoem

Companion
PRESS

All publications can be ordered by mail from:

Companion Press

3735 Broken Bow Road
Fort Collins, CO 80526

Phone: (970) 226-6050
Fax: 1-800-922-6051

www.centerforloss.com

Throughout the book, the theme of butterflies reminds readers that just as butterflies go through metamorphosis, so do grieving children. Activities are in an easy-to-follow format, each with a goal, objective, sequential description of the activity, and a list of needed materials.

ISBN 978-1-61722-185-9 • 208 pages • softcover • $29.95

WHEN GRIEF IS COMPLICATED

Companioning You!
A Soulful Guide to Caring for Yourself While You Care for the Dying and the Bereaved

In this essential addition to the Companioning Series, Dr. Wolfelt applies the principles of companioning others to the art of caring for yourself. Yes, caring for the dying and the bereaved is a rewarding ministry, but caregivers risk burnout and putting their own needs and lives last.

This book affirms the caregiver's right to excellent self-care and provides not only the rationale but the tips and practical suggestions you need to be your own friend and hospitable companion.

ISBN 978-1-61722-166-8 • 128 pages • hardcover • $15.95

Companion
PRESS

All publications can be ordered by mail from:

Companion Press

3735 Broken Bow Road
Fort Collins, CO 80526

Phone: (970) 226-6050
Fax: 1-800-922-6051

www.centerforloss.com

About the Author

Dr. Alan Wolfelt is an internationally noted author, educator, and grief counselor. Known for his model of "companioning" versus "treating," Dr. Wolfelt has become a "responsible rebel" who advocates for grief care that is compassionate, griever-led, and soul-

and spirit-based. Over the course of 40 years in clinical practice, he has helped thousands of grievers and developed a passionate interest in advocating for those experiencing complicated grief. This book adds his experienced voice to the literature on this challenging topic.

Past recipient of the Association of Death Education and Counseling's Death Educator Award, Dr. Wolfelt is an educational consultant to hospices, hospitals, schools, universities, funeral homes, and a variety of other community agencies across North America and around the world. Dr. Wolfelt also serves as Director of the Center for Loss and Life Transition and is on the faculty at the University of Colorado Medical School's Department of Family Medicine.

Dr. Wolfelt and his wife, Sue, have three grown children and live next door to the Center for Loss in Fort Collins, Colorado.